The **vodafone** Book of

‘Derby Quotations’

The vodafone Book of 'Derby Quotations'

Edited by

Laurie Brannan

vodafone

First published in Great Britain 2004
by Sportsguide Press, Crowthorne, Berkshire
info@sportsguidelimited.com

ISBN 0 954 47102 4

Printed and bound in Great Britain by Creative Print and Design

Designed and typeset by John Schwartz

Contents

“The wisdom of the wise and the experience of the ages are perpetuated by quotations.”

BENJAMIN DISRAELI (1804 –1881)

Foreword

THE EARL OF DERBY

'Derby'.

There's not a more famous single word in world sport. Not far from where I write these words, Liverpool play Everton at least twice a year in a local derby. Hickstead, home of show jumping, stages the British Jumping Derby. Then there's the Greyhound Derby . . .

All these uses of the word spring, of course, from the world's most famous horse race, first run in 1780 and named after my distinguished ancestor the 12th Earl. The Derby it was then, and the Derby it remains: to quote Paul Haigh, one of the many distinguished writers represented in the pages that follow, 'There is no such race as the Epsom Derby. What's run at Epsom is the Derby; its imitators are the ones that require geographical qualifiers.'

From the very start, the Derby took a hold on the public imagination, and generation after generation the race seems uncannily to represent the mood of the age, a microcosm of British society, high and low, brought together once a year for one all-embracing occasion.

So it is entirely appropriate that in the modern age the race should be sponsored, and sponsored so enthusiastically, by Vodafone, a company at the leading edge of a branch of communications technology which would have boggled the minds of Derby Day racegoers even twenty years ago – never mind what the 12th Earl would have made of it!

This wonderful book of Derby quotations, so painstakingly yet affectionately put together by Laurie Brannan, reflects the Derby in all its kaleidoscope of moods – triumph and disaster, virtue and skulduggery, winning and losing.

It serves as a permanent reminder of the unique place of that one five-letter word, not only in British life but in the lexicon of the whole sporting world: 'Derby'.

EARL OF DERBY
May 2004

Introduction

LAURIE BRANNAN

The inaugural running of the Derby on 4 May 1780 was, in truth, a low-key affair. The opening race on the day's programme, The Derby Stakes was contested by nine colts who competed for the 1,075-guinea sweepstakes and few who saw Sir Charles Bunbury's Diomed stride to victory that early English summer's day could possibly have imagined that the concept would become so successful that it would be copied more than two hundred times in countries around the world.

The seeds, though, for what was to become known as racing's Blue Riband were sown long before Diomed's historic victory. For without a certain Henry Whicker, a seventeenth-century herdsman, it is unlikely that racing would have come to Epsom. In 1618 Whicker struck upon a spring high on the Surrey Downs during a drought. Sadly for his cattle the water was of a strange taste and, despite the arid conditions, they refused to drink it. But the true qualities of Epsom's curious water lay undiscovered until 1632, when a group of labourers drank from Whicker's Well and in just a matter of hours were rendered prostrate by its medicinal properties.

Thus were discovered Epsom Salts, the efficacy of which as a rigorous and effective purgative, quickly spread to surrounding areas and transformed the once sleepy rural village into a thriving and bustling town. For a time, Epsom replaced Tunbridge Wells as the country's foremost spa, and, located less than a day's journey from the capital, it soon became a flourishing London retreat, with hunting, hawking and horse racing becoming part of the growing number of ancillary attractions. Charles II was a regular visitor to the area, and by the time Epsom's star began to fade as a recreational diversion in the eighteenth century, the town had firmly established itself as one of the country's principal locations for horse racing.

Originally a mile, the Derby's distance was increased in 1784 to a mile and a half, a trip considered to be the optimum test for three-year-old Thoroughbreds. The race soon became regarded as one of the Turf's principal contests, and with racing assuming a position as the country's pre-eminent sport, the Derby installed itself as an event of great national importance. Consequently, throughout its illustrious history, the Derby has acted as a social mirror, often reflecting the country's attitudes and values.

The late eighteenth century was the age of the aristocracy. It was a time when the nobility dominated both the nation's political and cultural spheres. The upper classes amassed enormous fortunes, allowing them to indulge in their passions, which for many was racing. A glance down the Derby's roll of honour shows that of the first twenty winners, fourteen were owned by the titled gentry, while in 1788 Sir Thomas provided a first win for royalty, carrying the colours of HRH the Prince of Wales to victory.

Pre-Victorian Britain was beset by loose morals, and racing was not exempt. Despite the efforts of the Jockey Club as the sport's regulatory body, Epsom raceweek invariably heralded a crime wave of pick-pockets and robbers, and racing itself was the subject of a host of illicit actions. Derby Day had become notorious for riots and drunkenness, and when the newly crowned Queen Victoria made her first and only visit to the Derby in 1840 the reception she received lacked both enthusiasm and respect.

The mid-nineteenth century, however, was a time of great industrial and technological progress. Perhaps the most significant development of the century was the evolution of the railways, and the Derby was no different to the rest of society in reaping the enormous rewards from the advent of steam power. Racing was becoming more professional and no longer the recreation of a privileged few. The advent of the railways meant that horses from across Britain could travel freely to racecourses. Increasing industrialisation and strained working conditions exaggerated the need for a common public distraction. Run in midweek, the Derby proved the ideal source of entertainment, and with trains facilitating easy access to the course, the Derby was transformed from a high-class race meeting into 'Britain's Biggest Day Out'.

The second half of the nineteenth century saw an upturn in the country's fortunes. Britain led the world in industrialisation, the Empire consumed all that stood before it, Britannia ruled the waves, and in the sphere of sport the rest could only watch and admire. Hence it was not only to racing's absolute shock and disgust but to the entire nation's bewilderment when Gladiateur, owned by the Comte de Lagrange, son of one of Napoleon's generals, won the Derby of 1865. Not surprisingly, the victory was received with rapturous celebrations in France where the colt was accorded the nickname 'The Avenger of Waterloo.'

Just as industrialisation had opened up the domestic boundaries, so, too did it greatly expedite foreign travel. Transatlantic crossings in particular were rendered significantly easier, and it was not long before the Americans had their say in the Derby. When Iroquois provided Uncle Sam with his first win in 1881, such was importance of the occasion across the water that trading was temporarily suspended on Wall Street.

While physical boundaries were being broken due to advances in travel, social barriers were being pushed to their limits. The Derby was also changing and no longer was it simply the greatest race in Britain, but an event with a place on the global calendar. So when suffragette, Emily Wilding Davison elected to throw herself under the hooves of the King's horse Anmer as he rounded Tattenham Corner in 1913, not only was she making a domestic protest, but she had chosen the world's largest stage to make a stand for women everywhere. The demand for news and information on the Derby became so insatiable that the result of Captain Cuttle's victory in 1922 was known in Australia just three minutes after Lord Woolavington's colt had crossed the finish line.

The Derby embraced technological advances. With moving pictures of the race having been taken in 1895. The Derby's ability to generate broad and popular appeal received an enormous boost when it was covered on the radio for the first time by the BBC in 1927, and by 1946 the race was available on domestic television sets.

The outbreak of the Great War put the Derby firmly in context. Suddenly the outcome of a horse race seemed less important and in 1915 Epsom racecourse was requisitioned by the military. Substitute Derbys were run at Newmarket but captured little imagination in a country ravaged by war. The Derby of 1917 was not run until July 31 as Parliament had suspended the sport earlier in the year due to lack of supplies. Racing historian Roger Mortimer captured the mood of the nation when he wrote: '1917 was a sombre year. Casualties had been on an appalling scale and the Somme battle the previous summer had thrown half the nation into mourning. The shipping position was causing the gravest anxiety, the Russians were cracking, and the end of the war seemed a long way off.'

Some twenty years later when the Second World War broke out, racing at Epsom was again suspended and the Derby reverted to Newmarket. This time, though, the mood of the nation was very different. Society in 1940 was bolstered with a sense of defiance and Mortimer records how the Derby reflected this spirit, writing, 'The extraordinary thing about the Derby of 1940 was the fact that it took place at all, coinciding as it did with the disintegration of French resistance, and the evacuation, less arms and equipment, of the British Expeditionary Force from Dunkirk. Yet at this moment of national peril, some thousands of people had the time and inclination to go racing, a tribute to national imperturbability in the face of crisis.'

The post-war era saw the emergence of the global village, and as countries throughout the world became increasingly cosmopolitan, so too did the Derby. In 1961 the shock win of 66-1 outsider Psidium, who was bred in Ireland out of an Italian mare, was owned by the wife of a Hungarian financier and ridden by a French jockey, marked the start of a fresh phase in the history of the great race. The emergence of Ireland, and the Coolmore Stud in particular, along with the Maktoum family as new racing empires greatly shifted the balance of power within the sport. As one of the racing's stellar prizes, the Derby has been at the forefront of the ambitions of these new conglomerates, and consequently the race has had huge international influence in recent decades.

An estimable tradition, which at one time prompted the suspension of Parliament for the day, the Derby never disappoints, producing a story year after year after year. It has seen many changes, but few have created more debate than the switch of the race from its traditional date on the first Wednesday in June to Saturday. Once again, it was a change in the nation's work ethic which dictated the move, with Margaret Thatcher's Britain becoming ruthlessly competitive.

The race began to die, with attendances dropping dramatically. Its demise was brought to a halt in 1995 when, with a new sponsor in telecommunications giant Vodafone, a substantial lift in prize money and run on a day of the week which ostensibly held greater public appeal, the Derby began a new, exciting and vibrant era.

* * *

The notion for a book of quotations on the Derby was conceived during a post-racing conversation with Vodafone's Group Corporate Affairs Director, Tim Brown, on Vodafone Oaks day in 2003. Its publication was planned to coincide with two significant milestones – the 225th running of the Derby and the tenth anniversary of Vodafone's sponsorship of the race. These factors, combined with the coincidence that Vodafone's internationally recognised icon is the quotation mark, suggested a certain simplicity in the concept, soon to evaporate as the complexity of the subject and its recognition at all levels in so many cultures began to emerge.

Sincere thanks are due to racing historian Sean Magee, not just for his help in gathering so many of the quotes, but also for his constructive advice in developing and shaping the text, to Jonathon Bates, who did a great deal of the research and remained enthusiastic throughout the project, and journalist John Randall whose diligence in checking the text has been invaluable. I am asked to say that 'Bernard Parkin made the drawings' rather than 'Drawings by Bernard Parkin' by Bernard himself, and I am pleased to acknowledge such a huge talent with so small a concession.

ONE

The Derby Dream

The Owners

‘As Persimmon walked back towards the unsaddling enclosure, the Downs echoed from one end to the other with cheers that were renewed again and again. Even the most dignified of individuals in the stands for once really let themselves go, and it was a truly remarkable exhibition of spontaneous enthusiasm and delight . . . The cheering reached its peak as the Prince came out to lead his horse in, and all in all it was a scene that could never be forgotten by those who saw it.’

Racing historian ROGER MORTIMER recalling the jubilation that greeted the Prince of Wales's 1896 Derby winner, Persimmon.

‘Hermit's Derby broke my heart. But I didn't show it, did I?’

THE MARQUIS OF HASTINGS, who heavily laid Hermit, shock winner of the 1867 Derby

‘There's only one race greater than the Jews – that's the Derby.’

SIR VICTOR SASSOON, owner of four Derby winners in eight runnings: Pinza (1953), Crepello (1957), Hard Ridden (1958) and St Paddy (1960)

‘Queen Victoria, who did not follow racing, attempted to congratulate him [two-time winner, Prime Minister Lord Rosebery] at one of her audiences but spoiled the effect by assuming that his consecutive victories were with the same horse.’

Author and broadcaster ALASTAIR BURNET.

Landmarks and Legends 1780

FIRST RUNNING OF THE DERBY STAKES ON 4 MAY, OVER ONE MILE, WITH PRIZE MONEY OF 1,075 GUINEAS.

‘In what are ecstatic moments for the few men lucky enough to own a Derby winner, he displayed not the slightest sign of pleasure while persisting in his refusal to lead in Merry Hampton.’

Journalist and racing historian RICHARD ONSLOW on George Alexander Baird's reaction to winning the 1887 Derby.

❛ Christmas came early for 83-year-old owner John Ismay when his colt Santa Claus won the Derby at Epsom yesterday. ❜

SHEFFIELD MORNING TELEGRAPH, 1964.

❛ He became favourite for the Derbv but at the same time I don't feel any confidence in him. ❜

The 17th EARL OF DERBY writing to a friend three weeks before his Hyperion won the 1933 Derby.

❛ John Bowes, son of the Earl and Countess of Strathmore, who forfeited the title, having been born before their marriage, was one of the outstanding owners of the middle nineteenth century years, with four Derby victors. Extremely wealthy, his attitude to the races was cavalier – for example, when he won £30,000 on West Australian in 1853, he did not bother to see him run. ❜

PATRICIA CONNOR and LIONEL LAMBOURNE, 1979.

❛ The Prince [of Wales] was a regular visitor to the Derby after his first visit in 1863. But he did not begin flat racing as an owner until 1877, and had no horses of classic standard until the 1890s. When his horse Persimmon won in 1896, its popularity rocketed it to fame. It became a cult figure, on a par with a modern television star, or the greatest steeplechasers (Arkle and Red Rum) of today. ’

PATRICIA CONNOR and LIONEL LAMBOURNE, 1979.

‘ Perhaps the trials don't tell us as much as they used to. Perhaps the Guineas has taken the place of the trials, we certainly look at it that way. ’

Owner–breeder JOHN MAGNIER, 2002.

‘ There was an interesting little sequel to the race that showed that 'The first Dictator of the Turf', like so many rich men, had a curious streak of meanness about his character. After the Derby a bookmaker called Brograve, unable to meet his creditors of whom Sir Charles [Bunbury] was one, saw fit to shoot himself. Sir Charles, therefore, handed Goodisson [Smolensko's jockey] three ten-pound notes for his three victories on Smolensko, explaining that owing to Brograve's default, he was unfortunately unable to afford any more. ’

Racing historian ROGER MORTIMER revealing the darker side of Smolensko's owner Sir Charles Bunbury, following the colt's victory in the 1813 Derby.

❛ *It is the Derby Wednesday, carrier pigeons come in flights,*
There is terror in St James's Street, and agony in White's.
From Hayling Isle to Newmarket they have begun to toast,
The foremost horse that stayed the course and foremost past the post. ❜

Opening verse of an ode by the fifth EARL OF ROSEBERY, predicting the running of the Derby in 1869, in which his horse Ladas finished last, but he won the Derby with another Ladas in 1894, and again with Sir Visto the following year.

Landmarks and Legends 1783

PHOENOMENON, WHO FINISHED LAST IN THE DERBY, WENT ON TO WIN THE ST LEGER AT DONCASTER AND BECAME THE FIRST HORSE TO RUN IN BOTH RACES.

❛ It is vulgar to win the Derby two years running. ❜

Owner LORD WEINSTOCK.

❛ Some of Lord Egremont's [Derby] winners were almost certainly four, not because their owner was greedy or dishonest but because his stud was conducted in a thoroughly haphazard manner. ❜

Historian ROGER MORTIMER'S assesment of the Derby record of the 3rd Earl of Egremont's (d. 1837).

Landmarks and Legends 1784

DISTANCE OF THE DERBY IS INCREASED TO ONE AND A HALF MILES.

❛ The scene after the Derby was a most remarkable and gratifying sight. ❜

Telegram sent by the PRINCE OF WALES to his mother, Queen Victoria, after his colt Persimmon had won the 1896 Derby.

❛ News of Diamond Jubilee's victory was communicated to me by Stanley during the attack on Brandfort yesterday. Army in South Africa beg to offer respectful congratulations. ❜

Telegram sent by LORD ROBERTS to the Prince of Wales following the victory of Diamond Jubilee in the 1900 Derby.

For the past 50 years the winning owner, almost without exception, had been a member of the aristocracy – wealthy, affluent and influential. For a slightly comical foreigner, whose English vocabulary was limited, to win the Derby became an unprecedented event.

Racing historian MICHAEL SETH-SMITH noting that in the context of the era Chevalier Ginistrelli's 1908 Derby win with Signorinetta was a startling achievement.

The reason why the Israelites found themselves in the rich and fertile plains of Jordan was that they followed manna. My advice to you is to do the same.

Prophetic advice given by HENRY MORRISS, owner of the 1925 Derby winner Manna, to guests attending the annual Press Luncheon on the eve of the race.

It is rather singular that the first Derby run over the new course should be won by a horse bred and named by Lord George Bentinck, by whom it was suggested and laid out; and not a little odd too, that the noble lord, who is remarkable for his punctuality in all things, should have arrived four minutes too late to see the race run.

THE TIMES raises an eyebrow at the circumstances of the 1848 Derby.

After trying to win the Derby for 137 years, victory in the historic race at Epsom was obtained yesterday by the House of Stanley. Lord Derby's colt Sansovino, outstripping all rivals, won by six lengths.

The *DAILY GRAPHIC*, 5 June, 1924, reporting on Lord Derby's victory.

Landmarks and Legends 1785

LORD CLERMONT BECOMES THE FIRST OWNER TO WIN BOTH THE DERBY AND THE OAKS IN THE SAME YEAR

When Galileo won last year I said things couldn't get any better, but this is just amazing.

Owner MICHAEL TABOR's reaction following High Chaparral's 2002 Vodafone Derby success.

An episode in the South African war makes me hope that this year – of all others – the Derby may be run. It was at the close of the first day's march of Lord Roberts' army from Johannesburg to Pretoria and the troops were just settling down into their bivouacs. Suddenly we saw heliographs flashing and mounted messengers galloping to the various units, their arrival being greeted by loud and prolonged cheering. When the message reached us it was found to be the following: 'The Field Marshal Commanding in Chief wishes it to be known to all ranks that the Prince of Wales's horse Diamond Jubilee has won the Derby.' I venture to think that Lord Roberts understood the British soldier better than those who are seeking to prevent the recurrence of such a scene as we witnessed that day. ❞

Letter from LORD ROSEBERY to *The Times* in 1915 when, with British troops fighting on the Continent, a debate was in progress as to whether the Derby should be run.

❝ There had always been rumours that if the teeth of some of Lord Egremont's Derby winners had been examined, they would have been found unnaturally long for three year-olds,

'Unnaturally Long'

and Bird, who trained for Lord Egremont, admitted on his death-bed that he had twice won the Derby with four year-olds through the simple expedient of slipping two year-olds into the yearling paddocks.

Historian ROGER MORTIMER, reflecting on the skulduggery that surrounded the Derby in its early days, points an accusing finger at Lord Egremont's trainer who won no fewer than five Derby's between 1782 and 1826

Landmarks and Legends 1787

THE FIRST DERBY FOR THE STANLEY FAMILY, WITH SIR PETER TEAZLE WINNING FOR THE TWELFTH EARL OF DERBY.

No thrill can ever match that of last Wednesday afternoon shortly after three o'clock when April the Fifth went past the post. I was bemused. I know not what I said, what I did. I am told that I did not cheer – I laughed aloud and then raced for the stairs . . . Just a few seconds before my horse passed the post I gave up hope. I saw him, seemingly hemmed in, without room to make his effort. I know I said aloud 'it is hopeless' and my glasses turned to the duel between Dastur and Miracle – I deserted my horse. Then suddenly I heard someone cry, 'What is that pink capped thing on the outside?' IT WAS MINE!

Actor, film star, bon viveur and owner–trainer TOM WALLS' whirlwind of emotions during April The Fifth's Derby win in 1932.

Landmarks and Legends 1788

SIR THOMAS, OWNED BY THE PRINCE OF WALES, IS THE FIRST ROYAL AND FIRST ODDS-ON WINNER.

In 1864 Chaplin [owner of the 1867 winner Hermit] was engaged to marry the beautiful Lady Florence Paget, but just before the wedding she jilted him and went off with the foolish, irresponsible, but far from unattractive Marquis of Hastings, a reckless gambler whose ruin was hastened by the gigantic losses he incurred over Hermit's astonishing victory at Epsom.

A case of poetic justice recalled by racing historian ROGER MORTIMER.

After an interval of 137 years the race was once again won by an Earl of Derby. The great crowd fully appreciated the significance of the occasion and, forgetting the miseries of one of the wettest afternoons in a deplorable summer, gave Lord Derby and his colt Sansovino a reception reminiscent of that accorded to King Edward and Minoru in 1909. ❞

Racing historian ROGER MORTIMER.

❝ We lost it on the nod. We were in front one stride before the line and one stride after. So we very nearly won the Derby. ❞

Owner PETER WINFIELD recalling how close his horse Silver Patriarch came to winning the 1997 Derby.

Landmarks and Legends 1794

THE SMALLEST DERBY FIELD EVER, WITH ONLY FOUR RUNNERS TAKING PART.

❝ My attitude, because I am a positive thinker, was that we nearly won. But what a gallant loser Silver Patriarch was. It certainly made the Derby for all those present and the millions who watched on television. My horse contributed to racing that day! ❞

Owner PETER WINFIELD still singing the praises of Silver Patriarch.

Landmarks and Legends 1798

SIR HARRY BECOMES THE FIRST DERBY WINER TO BE SIRED BY A PREVIOUS WINNER, SIR PETER TEAZLE.

❝ We took the private room at Annabel's and I had an arrangement with the Aga Khan, owner of Blushing Groom, that whoever won would host the dinner, and in the unlikely event of neither horse winning, we would go Dutch. Somebody was obviously convinced that Blushing Groom was going to win because they ordered all the flowers in the Aga's colours and had to switch them at the last moment. We had one hell of a party. ❞

Owner ROBERT SANGSTER recalling the celebrations after The Minstrel's 1977 Derby victory.

‘It’s like seeing your horse win the Derby, but carrying the Aga Khan’s colours.’

Journalist QUINTON GILBEY on seeing his son, who carried the name of his mother’s second husband, play for Eton at Lord’s, 1979.

Landmarks and Legends 1801

ELEANOR, WHO WON THE OAKS THE FOLLOWING DAY, BECOMES THE FIRST FILLY TO WIN THE DERBY.

‘It is the first instance of a man of rank and station in Society making such an exit.’

Diarist CHARLES GREVILLE writing about the Hon. Berkeley Craven, who shot himself rather than face the ignominy of failing to settle his bets after Bay Middleton had won the 1836 Derby.

‘The last few days before Epsom felt like the days before Christmas when I was a child.’

THE MARCHIONESS OF TAVISTOCK, 1993.

❛ I have left Oxford. I have secured a house in Berkeley Square; and I have bought a horse to win the Derby. ❜

Letter to his mother from the 5th EARL OF ROSEBERY.

❛ Only heaven left. ❜

Telegram from American CHAUNCEY DEPEW to the 5th Earl of Rosebery following his success with Ladas in the 1894 Derby.

❛ I am ashamed to have won the Derby thrice when so many owners have not won it once . . . ❜

The 5th EARL OF ROSEBERY.

❛ Dr Devious's owner was unusual: he ran one of the biggest slimming companies in the United States. So was his trainer: Chapple-Hyam had trained for just two years. And so was his jockey: John Reid was sufficiently unfashionable to have ridden his only classic winner ten years before. ❜

ALASTAIR BURNET on 1992 winner Dr Devious.

TWO

Immortality is Only a Heartbeat Away

The Trainers

❛ It's a great thrill, maybe the greatest, to win the Derby. I have been lucky enough to have won some big races all round the world, but there is something extra special about winning the Derby. ❜

SIR MICHAEL STOUTE, trainer of Derby winners Shergar (1981), Shahrastani (1986) and Kris Kin (2003).

❛ In the vivid green clamour of the paddock before the race, while the Derby runners parade, the owners and their wives, in top hats, morning coats and fashionable dresses, and the jockeys in their bright silks, can steal the scene and the public eye can overlook the man who has worked for two or three years to get the horse into that paddock, often the man with the anonymous face, who is a vital party of that trio. That man is the trainer. ❞

PATRICIA CONNOR and LIONEL LAMBOURNE, 1979.

'Overlooked'

❝ There are lots of other races around the world – like the Kentucky Derby, which is also a great race – but there's nothing like the Derby. ❞

AIDAN O'BRIEN, dual Vodafone Derby-winning Irish trainer.

❝ Darling was a martinet and a perfectionist, a cold man who cared little for human relationships but whose thoroughness and refusal to compromise brought him unprecedented success. ❜

Journalist JOHN RANDALL on trainer Fred Darling, who produced no fewer than seven Derby winners between 1922 and 1941.

❛ My advice to punters has always been to focus their resources on high-quality racing; it tends to be more profitable because every horse and jockey is trying its best and the form is more reliable. Yet, perversely, the English Derby, the so-called 'Blue Riband of the Turf,' which should turn out the top three-year-olds, has brought me as much despair as it has success. ❜

Legendary gambler and trainer BARNEY CURLEY.

'Despair': Barney Curley

‘In 1965 a weak heart ended my father Towser Gosden’s career as he nurtured the champion two-year-old Charlottown in his stable. My father retired in December but continued his involvement with Charlottown’s training and six months later Charlottown won the Derby – a unique bitter-sweet pill that undoubtedly hurried my father’s precipitously early death.’

Trainer JOHN GOSDEN’s poignant recollection of his father and Charlottown, 1997.

‘I rather looked upon Shergar’s win as a job completed, because he was the perfect athlete, eminently suited to the track, and everything went well with his preparation. He was just much too good for all of them, and when he won it was a feeling of relief as much as anything because everyone expected him to win.’

Trainer SIR MICHAEL STOUTE recalling Shergar’s 1981 Derby triumph by ten lengths.

Landmarks and Legends 1813

SMOLENSKO BECOMES THE FIRST BLACK HORSE TO WIN THE DERBY AND THE FIRST TO COMPLETE THE TWO THOUSAND GUINEAS AND DERBY DOUBLE.

They will tell you that for a trainer, big-race tension diminishes steadily, year by year, and there is only one thing wrong with that statement. It isn't true. Any Derby in which you have a fancied runner becomes a pretty tense affair and it doesn't get any easier with the passing years. It gets worse.

Trainer MARCUS MARSH from his autobiography *Racing with the Gods*, 1968.

For a trainer, it gets worse

The Derby remains the most prestigious event in the flat racing calendar, sustained by centuries of history and tradition. Our six winners of the race are an enduring source of pride, each evoking very different memories. From my first runner Ballymoss, who was second to Crepello in 1957, to my last, Fatherland [in 1993], the Derby has never failed to exert its magic. ’

Legendary Irish trainer VINCENT O'BRIEN.

‘ My one great failure as a trainer – I never made a gentleman of Lester Piggott. ’

JACK JARVIS, trainer of Derby winners Blue Peter (1939) and Ocean Swell (1944).

‘ When I got home there were banners on all the gates and 200 people in my home making their way through all my drink. The best thing, though, was riding out the following morning, looking out on the Downs and thinking who might be next year's Derbv horse. That, for me, sums up the fascination of the race. ’

PETER WALWYN, trainer of Grundy, describes the emotions of winning the 1975 Derby.

‘ I was sure we had a very good chance. The French Guineas winner, Green Dancer, started 6-4 favourite, but I trained No Alimony, who was third to him in the previous year's

Observer Gold Cup – and we knew Grundy was far superior to No Alimony. ❞

Trainer PETER WALWYN had good reason to be confident of winning in 1975.

❝ 'Thank God and you sir,' an old woman said to his trainer on his return in triumph from Epsom, 'that we have lived to see a Catholic horse win the Derby'. ❞

After ORBY, trained by Colenal Frederick McCabe, had in 1907 become the first Irish-trained horse to win the Derby.

"Don't give him any to drink yet."

“Who says they cannot train a Derby winner in Epsom?”

Owner-trainer TOM WALLS’ proud boast following April The Fifth’s Derby success in 1932.

Landmarks and Legends 1821

GUSTAVUS BECOMES THE FIRST GREY TO WIN THE DERBY.

“Villainy on the Turf reached the depths of nefarious skulduggery in 1844 when the four year-old Running Rein was first past the post in the Derby and subsequently disqualified after an investigation and a court case that would have made a modern detective story seem second rate.”

Racing historian MICHAEL SETH-SMITH.

“My Derby winners were all very different in character. Slip Anchor was very hyper, but very good on his day. Reference Point was very, very lazy and had bad sinus trouble during his two-year-old career and so had to be operated on. I never got to the bottom of him. Commander In Chief had never run at two and I had to push him hard to get him into the Derby.

Oath was a grand little horse, very active and decent. I could have had another Derby winner, I believe, if Simply Great had not broken his leg a week before the [1982] race. ’

Trainer HENRY CECIL compares his four Derby winners.

Landmarks and Legends 1823

THE RACING CALENDAR AFFORDED THE WINNING JOCKEY THE HONOUR OF HAVING HIS NAME OFFICIALLY RECORDED FOR THE FIRST TIME.

‘ Right up to about a week before the Derby, we didn't know who was going to ride him. Then, having ridden work on him, Lester [Piggott] rang me and said, ‘I think I am going to ride your horse.’ I said, ‘Are you sure, now?’ Anyway, at the top of the Hill, I turned to the missus and said: ‘If he keeps on going like this, he'll trot up.’ ’

GEOFF WRAGG, trainer of the 1983 Derby winner Teenoso.

‘ I was hoping that Benny [The Dip] might be placed, but, like so many, I thought it was just a case of what would be second to Entrepreneur. However, when I saw Mick Kinane's elbows start pumping running down the hill I knew Entrepreneur was in trouble. Mick could not get the favourite to go and I thought we might yet be in business. Willie [Ryan] had kicked on Benny, but when I looked back through the field I could see this big grey [Silver Patriarch] closing down on us, with Pat Eddery clearly smelling the scent of victory in his nostrils. I was sure we'd get caught, but Benny dug in again when the other fellow got upsides, and he got there on the nod. ❜

Trainer JOHN GOSDEN describing the closing stages of the 1997 Derby.

❛ It would have been nice to spend a few days celebrating, but unfortunately life goes on – you have to be up for first lot the next morning. ❜

Trainer LUCA CUMANI, who was unable to let his hair down after the 1988 Derby success of Kahyasi. He won the race again ten years later with High-Rise.

❛ The actual day at Epsom was all a bit of a rush. Tea with the Queen, meet the sponsors, talk to the press. On the way home, the phone never stopped ringing, and there were local radio and papers to greet us when we got out of the car – and a lot of home-made bunting, all looking rather tacky! ❜

Trainer ROGER CHARLTON on Quest For Fame's 1990 victory.

THREE

A Race For Legends

The Jockeys

My first Derby experience, at the age of fifteen back in pre-starting stalls days of 1951, could hardly have worked out worse. Zucchero was a notoriously difficult horse and showed no sense of Derby Day occasion, digging his toes in as the tapes went up. When he finally consented to go, his rivals were halfway over the horizon, and that was that.

Record nine times Derby winning jockey LESTER PIGGOTT
recalling a disappointing Derby debut.

The supreme satisfaction of riding a Derby winner has eluded many gifted and otherwise successful jockeys throughout their career. Yet on Derby Day 1923, the main point of interest was whether Stephen Donoghue could ride the winner for the third year in succession. ’

Derby archivist GEORGE MELTON.

Landmarks and Legends 1827

FIRST DERBY RACECARD PRODUCED BY WILLIAM DORLING, CLERK OF THE COURSE.

‘ In the years when the BBC was covering the Derby in competition with ITV, I would be sited on a rostrum by the Rubbing Horse public house, about 100 yards beyond the winning post. Talk about boxing with your hands tied behind your back! Nonetheless, I got the first interview post-race with Lester [Piggott] after his wins on both Nijinsky and Roberto. We had an arrangement and Lester delivered. He was totally professional and reliable. ’

Former BBC television racing front man JULIAN WILSON.

‘ Close home, I knew one was coming and all I could think was where the bloody winning post was. When I saw the grey head of Silver Patriarch alongside me I can't tell you what I thought. It had been a dream from an early age to win the Derby, but it was a relief as losing in those circumstances would have been a big let-down. ’

Jockey WILLIE RYAN recalls his narrow victory in the 1997 Vodafone Derby on Benny The Dip.

Landmarks and Legends 1828

THE FIRST DEAD-HEAT AND THE FIRST AND LAST RUN-OFF TO DECIDE THE WINNER. CADLAND BEAT THE COLONEL.

‘ There is a physical as well as spiritual side to Steve [Donoghue]'s success. It is called balance. Watch him come down the hill at Epsom. You never see him holding onto the reins as many of his colleagues are compelled to. His touch downhill is as light as it is on the flat, and that I believe is why he is so successful on the Downs course. His mounts have never any shifting dead weight to carry. ’

Newspaper eulogy following STEVE DONOGHUE's sixth Derby victory in 1925 on Manna.

❛ It's always special to win the Derby. You can never believe it when it happens. ❜

KIEREN FALLON, rider of Vodafone Derby winners Oath (1999) and Kris Kin (2003).

❛ You have to keep your horse relaxed so you go into the stalls as quietly as possible. Stalls 10 and 13 seem to be lucky ones. ❜

Four times Derby-winning jockey WILLIE CARSON.

Landmarks and Legends 1829

A POLICEMAN VISITED THE DERBY IN AN OFFICIAL CAPACITY FOR THE FIRST TIME. HE CHARGED £7 FOR THE SERVICES OF HIMSELF AND HIS AIDES.

❛ My normal Derby strategy was fairly simple: lay up handy in the early stages, a few places off the leaders, and never get too far behind. The ideal is to be about fourth or fifth at Tattenham Corner, get your horse balanced once straightened up for home, and then work your way into a challenging position.'

LESTER PIGGOTT, greatest of all Derby jockeys.

'One thing you've got to have at Epsom is confidence – you've got to have a lot of confidence – you've got to know you must not allow things to worry you, and when you walk into the weighing room you can see that most of the jockeys are worried stiff.'

Three times winning jockey HARRY WRAGG on how he loved riding at Epsom, especially on Derby Day.

'worried stiff'

'One evening in May 1985, dining with Steve Cauthen in Pontevecchio, Steve bet me £50 that, if the going was 'firm', Slip Anchor would win the Derby by five lengths! That was how confident the man was. In the event, the going was good and Slip Anchor won by seven lengths. ❞

Former BBC television's racing front man JULIAN WILSON.

❝ Michael Stoute took me to see Harry Wragg before Shergar's Derby and he said that the inside rail was the best place to be, to keep a cool head and get your horse up the hill in one piece. At the top of the hill the dead wood starts to come back and by that stage you want to be picking two or three out and setting yourself a target. All my best rides in the Derby came when I was on the rail or one off it. If I was further out than that, I never figured. There is a lot of buffeting and if you're on the rail they can only get you from one side. ❞

Triple Derby-winning jockey WALTER SWINBURN.

❝ Once you've won it, you want to win it again, probably even more so because you know how it feels. ❞

Jockey WILLIE RYAN, rider of 1997 Vodafone Derby winner Benny The Dip.

❝ As Gordon rode back in triumph to the incessant roars of the crowd his face was impassive – outwardly hiding his innermost knowledge that his heart was pounding with excitement. ❞

Broadcaster and racing historian MICHAEL SETH-SMITH in *Knight of the Turf* (1980) describing Sir Gordon Richards' 1953 triumph on Pinza.

❝ Coming into Tattenham Corner, there is a huge crowd on the infield and on the other side of the rails. Either side, there are people screaming, and you can hear the roar. It's like running down a tunnel of noise. Now you know whether your horse is in the race. The ground is dropping away and horses don't like it – they don't understand what's happening. Some of them have never galloped downhill before and you are keeping hold of their heads. Everyone's thinking this is it! ❞

Jockey WILLIE CARSON's spine-tingling recollection of riding round Tattenham Corner.

❝ Some have said the Derby is not the race it once was – believe me, it is the race that every jockey wants to win. ❞

Dual Vodafone Derby winning rider JOHNNY MURTAGH, 2002.

❝ The Derby of 1885 provided one of the most thrilling finishes in the history of the race, and Melton's victory by a head over Paradox was in no small measure due to the wonderful riding of Fred Archer. ’

Racing historian ROGER MORTIMER underlining that Fred Archer was the greatest jockey of his generation.

‘ I had switched him off too much, but once he woke up, it was easy. ’

LESTER PIGGOTT reflecting on Nijinsky's 1970 Derby triumph.

'Wake up!'

‘I must have been mad. Stark, staring mad. It was the morning of the Derby of 1939. I had the greatest chance ever of winning on Blue Peter, and there I was in the paddock of my father's farm, riding a hunter ‘over the sticks’.’

EPH SMITH in his autobiography *Riding to Win* (1968) commenting on his unorthodox preparation prior to winning the 1939 Derby.

Landmarks and Legends 1830

WHEN THE GRANDSTAND WAS OPENED, SUCH WAS THE PROBLEM OF CROWD CONTROL THAT MAGISTRATES WERE ADMITTED FREE AND A ROOM SET ASIDE IN THE STAND FOR THE DETENTION OF PRISONERS.

‘I always tried to keep big races like the Derby on a business footing and maintain a sense of perspective. The most important thing is to think of it as just another race – emotion must not come into it.’

Jockey ERNIE JOHNSON, who won the 1969 Derby on Blakeney and three years later was beaten by a short head on Rhinegold.

I thought Sir Ivor wouldn't stay, but when I saw him there half a furlong out, although my chap was running on, I knew that we'd had it. He's the most brilliant horse I've ever seen in all my nineteen years!

SANDY BARCLAY, rider of Connaught, runner-up in the 1968 Derby.

Landmarks and Legends 1831

THIS YEAR SAW A CHANGE IN THE RACE CONDITIONS WHICH REQUIRED THE OWNER OF THE WINNER TO PROVIDE £100 TOWARDS THE EXPENSES OF THE POLICE AND, INSTEAD OF RECEIVING £100 OUT OF THE STAKES, THE OWNER OF THE SECOND WAS TO SAVE HIS STAKE OF £50.

I felt myself beginning to be overcome by the knowledge of what had just taken place. In order to return to the unsaddling enclosure before the tears of joy ran down my face, I did my best to think of anything but the fact that my ultimate dream had just come true. It is difficult to put into words the elation I felt at that time – it was, of course, simply the pinnacle of my career.

Jockey EDWARD HIDE in his autobiography *Nothing to Hide* (1989) on his reaction to winning the 1973 Derby on Morston.

❛ You have always to respect any Derby winner – there's no such thing as a bad one. ❜

Jockey FRANKIE DETTORI, 2003.

❛ In 1824 Jem Robinson brought off a remarkable wager, having betted that in one week he would ride the winner of the Derby, the winner of the Oaks, and get married. He won the Derby on Sir John Shelley's Cedric, the Oaks on Lord Jersey's Cobweb, and on the Saturday he completed the treble by leading a certain Miss Powell to the altar. ❜

Historian ROGER MORTIMER records an a amazing treble.

❛ There's no particular skill required in riding the Derby – just balance. ❜

Nine times Derby-winning rider LESTER PIGGOTT.

'Just balance!'

❛ The Epsom Derby is a fantastic race to win for any jockey, the greatest in the world. It's the race for legends. I've won many of the biggest races in the world, but when you tell people about them, the one they have heard of is the Epsom Derby. People in England love their racing and everyone knows the Derby. ❜

OLIVIER PESLIER, rider of 1998 Vodafone Derby winner High-Rise.

Landmarks and Legends 1832

THE WINNER ST GILES, OF WHOM IT WAS COMMONLY ALLEGED THAT HE WAS A FOUR-YEAR-OLD, WON HIS OWNERS MORE THEN £100,000 IN BETS.

❛ It's a great feeling to win the Derby. This is the race we all want to win. I said at the start of the year I'd be happy to win a Classic, and now I've a Guineas and a Derby. It couldn't be better. The Derby is the greatest race. ❜

KIEREN FALLON following his success on the 2003 Vodafone Derby winner Kris Kin.

❛If you look at Lester [Piggott]'s Derby rides, up the hill, where he was sat, he stayed. He always conserved his horse. If you get to the top of the hill in one piece, that's the first and probably most important stage over.❜

Triple Derby-winning jockey WALTER SWINBURN.

❛The Derby is everybody's dream. I have won nine Classics, but not the Derby. The best three-year-olds, best jockeys, best trainers and the best owners have won it and I haven't. So it is very important for me to try and win it, to complete my career and complete my job as a professional jockey.❜

Jockey FRANKIE DETTORI.

'This is nothing! Wait till I win the Derby'

“I’ve been fortunate to win a race at the Breeders’ Cup, but there’s nothing quite like the Derby. From when you’re a kid in short trousers you wonder what it’s like to win the Derby. And now I’ve done it, I can tell you there’s no feeling quite like it.”

JOHNNY MURTAGH after riding Sinndar to win the Vodafone Derby in 2000.

Landmarks and Legends 1835

MUNDIG WAS THE FIRST OF FOUR DERBY WINNERS FOR OWNER JOHN BOWES, WHO WAS ONLY TWENTY-ONE AT THE TIME AND STILL A STUDENT AT CAMBRIDGE.

“At Tattenham Corner Archer spotted the slenderest of openings on the rails and through it he drove the favourite though he had to lift his left leg to the level of Bend Or’s head to prevent it from being crushed.”

Racing historian ROGER MORTIMER recounts the daring of jockey Fred Archer in winning the 1880 Derby on Bend Or.

❛ A thousand pounds for a pull! ❜

Jockey BILL SCOTT's ignored plea to fellow rider Macdonald as he swept past the favourite Launcelot to win the 1840 Derby on Little Wonder.

❛ I don't care how experienced a jockey is - if he says he is not nervous when facing up to riding in the biggest and oldest classic of them all, he is lying. ❜

Triple Derby-winning rider PAT EDDERY, 2003.

❛ He went so wide that he appeared desirous of visiting relatives in Putney. ❜

Journalist and historian ROGER MORTIMER recalling Freddie Head coming round Tattenham Corner on Lyphard in the 1972 Derby.

❛ The Derby, aye! with twenty-three good ones (if one may believe all that is said and done), all ready to start, and all 'sure to win', enough, really, to make one breathless to think of it. But a drenching shower, thirteen false starts, and an hour (or nearly so) later than expected, gave time for the jockey, with his tiffany silk jacket and muslin shirt, to get dry again; for the heaving bosom to become tranquil, and for him who had a good horse, in his own imagination only, to begin to waver. ❞

BEN MARSHALL, painter and sporting journalist, describing the 1830 Derby won by Priam.

❝ The reason why [Steve] Donoghue always distinguished himself at Epsom is that he is so clever at getting off and gets going so well that he is rarely if ever bunched in going downhill. ❞

GEORGE DULLER, famed hurdle rider, 1922.

❝ The way to win the Derby is to get on the best horse and ride as if it was just another one and a half mile race at Epsom, provided the other jockeys will let you, which, of course, they won't. ❞

JACK LEACH, jockey, trainer and writer.

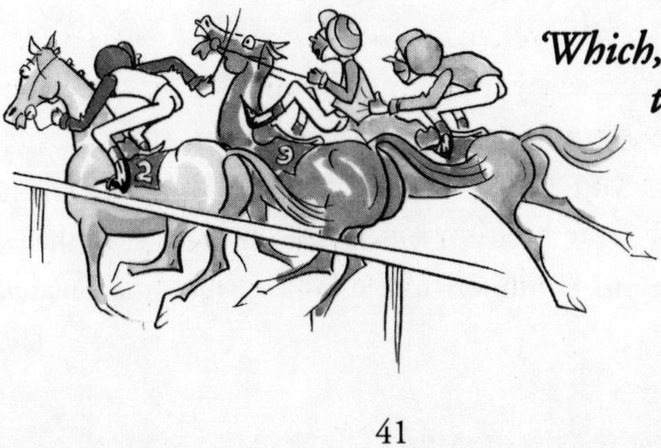

'Which, of course, they won't'

‘Willie Carson is as good a rider as there has been round Epsom. He used to give his horses time to build up and once they were ready then he started to put them into the race.’

Triple Derby winning rider WALTER SWINBURN, 1998.

‘Winning the Derby is the best feeling you get out of racing. It's the thing you've been striving for all your life – and it doesn't happen to many people.’

Jockey WILLIE CARSON

Landmarks and Legends 1837

THE FIRST DERBY TO BE STARTED BY FLAG AND THE LAST RUN ON A THURSDAY, THE RACE BEING SWITCHED TO WEDNESDAY THE FOLLOWING YEAR.

‘The Derby of 1812 was regrettably marred by foul play . . . Ridden by Sam Chifney junior, Manuella started second favourite at 7-2. Chifney, however, was not the first or the last great jockey to be thoroughly dishonest when the financial incentive was deemed sufficient, and he deliberately stopped the filly. The next day he booked a bet of 2,000 to 100 about her for the Oaks in which she was ridden by Pierce. She duly won that race. ❞

Foul play unearthed by historian ROGER MORTIMER.

❝ Buckle and I wound in and out all the way from Tattenham Corner like a dog at the fair. ❞

Jockey SAM DAY describing how he and Frank Buckle, the most famous rider of his day and five times winner of the Derby, were forced to dodge the litter on the course in 1821.

Landmarks and Legends 1838

AMATO BECOMES THE FIRST EPSOM-TRAINED WINNER OF THE DERBY IN THE YEAR THAT SPECIAL TRAIN SERVICES ARE INTRODUCED.

❝ Winning the Derby was the greatest feeling in the world, one of sheer elation. As I went past the post I felt that I had earned my place in the historv books even if I didn't achieve another thing in the future. ❞

Jockey ERNIE JOHNSON, who won the 1969 Derby on Blakeney.

❝ I was very confident. We won the Dante with so much in hand that I said to John [Dunlop] there and then that he [Shirley Heights] would win the Derby. ❞

Jockey GREVILLE STARKEY, who won the 1978 Derby on Shirley Heights.

❝ I have been told that my expression never changed, that I seemed to take that tremendous moment unnaturally quietly, even when I was being led in. This seems to have surprised some people, in view of the fact that I had just won my first Derby after all those years of disappointment. But I am not surprised myself. Frankly my mind was in turmoil, and my brain perhaps being a little numbed. Everyone was being so tremendously kind . . . ❞

SIR GORDON RICHARDS recounting his sole success in the Derby – at his twenty-eighth attempt – with Pinza in 1953.

❝ There has never been a better judge of pace, no greater student of the form book, no stronger finisher when ice-cool judgement, nerve and determination to make his mount give his all are desperately needed in the final strides before the winning-post is reached. ’

Racing historian MICHAEL SETH-SMITH acknowledging Lester Piggott as the greatest Derby jockey of them all.

‘ When the race starts, you don't blink, you don't even breathe for the whole of the two and a half minutes of the race. It is so intense. ’

Jockey's FRANKIE DETTORI.

Landmarks and Legends 1840

QUEEN VICTORIA ATTENDS THE DERBY FOR THE FIRST AND ONLY TIME, OFFICIALLY RECOGNISING THE RACE AS A NATIONAL OCCASION.

‘ To win it you need a horse that can adapt to the unusual conditions, an undulating mile and a half like no other race in the world. It's always highly competitive, with no quarter either asked or given. Essentially, you want a colt with a bit of pace who also stays. The pace gives him the ability to get out of trouble and to quicken when you straighten up. The stamina takes him to the line when some of the others have cried enough. ’

Jockey RICHARD QUINN.

Landmarks and Legends **1841**

THIS YEAR SEES A RECORD NUMBER OF RUNNERS IN THE DERBY WITH 29 GOING TO POST.

‘ Basically, you have got to be in touch with your horse and must not ask him to do something he is not capable of. He might not be able to lie up early on, he might be running too free. You must be in tune with your mount and nurse him round. ’

Jockey WALTER SWINBURN, 1998.

‘ On Derby Day itself, I didn't leave the weighing room until 7.30 p.m. When I did eventually get home, Lester [Piggott] had opened all my telegrams and read the lot. I lived only ten minutes from the course and we had quite a few friends around, including Lester and Jimmy Tarbuck. We had a full-scale celebration about three weeks later when I hosted a party for eighty people at the Dorchester. Tarby and the Joe Loss Orchestra did a cabaret for me. You don't win too manv Derbys and when you do, you have to push the boat out. ’

Jockey GEOFF LEWIS and the celebrations that followed Mill Reef's 1971 Derby win.

Landmarks and Legends 1843

JOCKEYS ARE WARNED THAT PENALTIES WILL BE IMPOSED FOR MISBEHAVIOUR AT THE START. FOR ONCE THERE IS NO DELAY IN DESPATCHING THE RUNNERS.

‘ I don't know why it should be so that French-trained horses have had such little success in the Derby over the years. I do know that French jockeys have always found the Derby course difficult to master if they haven't ridden there before, due to its turns and undulations. ’

YVES SAINT-MARTIN, fifteen times French champion and rider of 1963 Derby winner Relko.

❛ I was always confident Relko would win – and even took the day before the race off for a sightseeing trip, taking photos of the pigeons in Trafalgar Square. ❜

Jockey YVES SAINT-MARTIN, again.

❛ It is not just my dream – it is the dream of every jockey on the planet. Everybody wants to win the Epsom Derby because it is simply the best race in the world. ❜

Jockey FRANKIE DETTORI.

❛ The Derby is still the most important race in the world and any jockey would give his right arm to win it. My dream was to win the race, but then when I'd won it I wanted to win it again and again. ❜

Triple Derby winning rider PAT EDDERY

❛ You go into the race with a fixed plan, but it's rare that your best laid plans come off. ❜

WALTER SWINBURN, 1998.

❛ It was a marvellous day, and I only wish I had had more time to digest everything. I could not even have a drink with the Queen in the Royal Box, because I had to rush off to meet my helicopter down at the seven-furlong gate to fly to Ireland to ride at The Curragh that evening. I was on a terrific high, and then I got beat on Goodnight Kiss at 4-1 on. That really brought me back down to earth! ❜

MICK KINANE reflecting on his first Derby triumph on Commander In Chief in 1993.

❛ When [Alan] Munro received a four-day ban for careless riding at Goodwood, prohibiting his return to the saddle until Derby Day itself, it was not perhaps the best of omens. But Prince Fahd telephoned his new jockey to tell him not to worry and to treat the Derby as just another race. He need never have been concerned. A trained monkey could have won on Generous that day, so superior was he to the rest of his generation of three-year-old colts. ❜

Racing journalist COLIN MACKENZIE, 2001.

❛ [Fred] Archer, like Piggott, knew how to ride Epsom like none of his rivals did. He had a will of iron. It was said he would come round Tattenham Corner with one leg over the rail if he had to. ❞

ALASTAIR BURNET, 1993.

❝ I don't go along with Lester Piggott's philosophy that you have to be close to the leaders round Tattenham Corner. Plenty of good horses have come from way back. ❞

WALTER SWINBURN, 1998.

❝ It's just a race. ❞

LESTER PIGGOTT'S terse response to reporters when asked how it felt after winning the Derby for the first time on Never Say Die in 1954.

❝ The Derby has been a showcase for all the diverse talents of Lester Piggott in a way that no other race could have been. ❞

Racing journalist and historian RICHARD ONSLOW.

‘Nobody has ever understood the mystique of the Derby as comprehensively as Lester Piggott.’

Racing journalist and historian RICHARD ONSLOW.

‘When I won the Derby for the first time on Sinndar two years ago the feeling was one of total elation, but this time it was one of high emotion.’

Jockey JOHNNY MURTAGH following High Chaparral's 2002 Derby victory.

‘Unimaginative and singularly unmoved by the importance of the occasion – the Derby, except in cash value, probably means little more to him than a seller at Windsor – he is brilliant at the gate, always seems to have his mount in just the right position throughout the race, and is a very powerful finisher indeed. He is unquestionably the best Epsom rider of today.’

Racing historian ROGER MORTIMER'S view of Lester Piggott, 1963.

FOUR

The Supreme Test of the Thoroughbred

The Derby Horse and the Derby Course

"Sir Ivor in 1968 won with a sensational burst of speed which surprised even me, and Nijinsky was a horse you could put anywhere in a race and was thus an ideal Derby runner. In 1970 he showed his true class when beating Gyr, but in terms of overall ability I always rated Sir Ivor just superior, the greatest of my Derby winners."

Record nine times Derby-winning rider LESTER PIGGOTT

Landmarks and Legends 1844

THE HORSE FIRST PAST THE POST, RUNNING REIN, IS DISCOVERED TO BE THE FOUR-YEAR-OLD MACCABEUS.

‘Blakeney [who won in 1969] was a very laid-back horse who would only ever beat a plater by a neck at home. On Derby Day, he was ultra-calm and stood on three legs in the stalls.’

Jockey ERNIE JOHNSON.

Landmarks and Legends 1846

THE DERBY IS OFFICIALLY TIMED, PYRRHUS THE FIRST CLOCKING TWO MINUTES AND FIFTY-FIVE SECONDS.

‘Unique among Derby winners of my experience.’

Renowned racing journalist QUINTON GILBEY’s description of the 1965 Derby winner Sea-Bird.

‘Entering the final furlong, he [Troy] led by two lengths and he ran on so strongly that the winning margin was seven lengths. Spectators could hardly believe the evidence of their own eyes, for it is seldom that a Classic field is treated in the closing stages as if it were composed of horses more accustomed to performing at an evening meeting at Wolverhampton. ❞

Historian ROGER MORTIMER in praise of the 1979 Derby winner.

❝ It is the Epsom Derby which has made the Thoroughbred what it is today. ❞

Legendary Italian breeder FEDERICO TESIO – 1869–1954.

Landmarks and Legends 1847

DERBY DAY IS RECOGNISED BY PARLIAMENT AS A PUBLIC HOLIDAY. FIRST LOW-LEVEL START IS USED, AND A NEW RECORD OF 32 RUNNERS GO TO POST.

❝ It can be said that the Derby course and distance provide an admirable test of the Thoroughbred. A true-run mile and a half – there is seldom any loitering in the Derby – demands speed and stamina combined, and eliminates both the fast short-runner and the plodder devoid of acceleration. The gradients require from a horse the ability to race both uphill and down, and as a rule only a horse of good conformation can negotiate the steep descent to Tattenham Corner without becoming to some extent unbalanced. Competitors that are too straight in front or heavy in the shoulder are at a considerable disadvantage. Furthermore, the atmosphere of tension and excitement on Derby Day, the crowds that throng round a fanciered runner in the paddock, and above all the lengthy parade in front of the stands, combine to make the race a considerable test of temperament to win. ❜

Journalist and racing historian ROGER MORTIMER's definitive observations on the unique nature of the Derby course and the sort of horse it takes to win the race.

❛ A good Derby winner can sprint and stay a mile and a half. You are asking, therefore, for a very special, very peculiar type of animal. ❜

PETER BURRELL, Director of the National Stud.

'He's peculiar all right – but maybe a bit <u>too</u> peculiar?'

❛ The Thoroughbred exists because its selection has depended not on experts, technicians or zoologists, but one piece of wood: the winning post of the Epsom Derby. ❜

FEDERICO TESIO, Italian breeder.

Landmarks and Legends **1848**

THE DERBY START IS MOVED TO LANGLEY BOTTOM TO ENABLE GRANDSTAND PATRONS TO SEE IT.

❛ The title of Derby winner still conveys great distinction and, like the race itself, those that lead the great scamper down Tattenham Corner and up the cambered Surrey downs can become part of the vernacular. ❜

Journalist RICHARD EDMONDSON, 2003.

❛ Sea Bird II had treated his opponents as though they were so many selling platers, a fact that led many commentators to lament over the standard of the rest of the Derby field. But to malign the vanquished was to detract from the merit of the victor . . . The opposition to Sea Bird wasn't bad, it's just that Sea Bird made it *look* bad – the hallmark of a truly great horse! ❞

Timeform's *RACEHORSES OF 1965.*

Landmarks and Legends 1849

DERBY PRIZE MONEY OF £6,325 TO THE WINNER SETS A NEW RECORD.

❝ It is a singular anomaly that the greatest race in the world should be run over perhaps the worst and most dangerous course that we have. The elder trainers and jockey may well sigh for the days of the Old Derby course, with its nice gentle rise of three quarters of a mile, which nearly settled the thing before Tattenham Corner. All that is changed now. However the Grandstand folk like to see the race end to end, and they must have their way. ❞

The alteration of the Derby course in 1848 did not meet with unanimous approval, as one anonymous correspondent wrote.

❛ If ever a horse looked like a Derby winner in the paddock before the race, it was Hyperion. In size he was little more than a pony, but in proportion he was magnificent.

Derby archivist GEORGE MELTON.

Landmarks and Legends 1851

THE DERBY FIELD OF THIRTY-THREE CONSTITUTES A FRESH RECORD FOR THE RACE.

❛ I understand that Milton's *Paradise Lost* is being revived and will appear in Derby week and will be published under the title *Paradox Lost* by Melton. ❜

Telegram sent by OSCAR WILDE to Lord Hastings after his horse Paradox had been beaten by Melton in the 1885 Derby.

❛ Nijinsky's year was a very special one, with the unbeaten champion ridden by Lester Piggott and trained by Vincent O'Brien. For me, watching from the old press stand at the top of the grandstand, it was a thrill never to be forgotten seeing this great partnership swoop on the French colts Gyr and Stintino; but my memory also recalls the massive lines of open-top buses and the crowds which flocked on to the hill from soon after first light to get a view of the race. ❞

Journalist TONY STAFFORD recalls a memorable Derby.

Landmarks and Legends 1853

THE DERBY IS WON BY THE 2,000 GUINEAS WINNER WEST AUSTRALIAN, WHO GOES ON TO TAKE THE ST LEGER AND THUS BECOME THE FIRST WINNER OF THE TRIPLE CROWN.

❝ Fortunately nobody knows how to breed a Derby winner. If they did, it would take all the fun out of it. ❞

JAMES WEATHERBY.

❝ The main aim of the Queen's breeding operation has always been to produce a winner of the Derby, the only domestic Classic she has never won . . . The likelihood is that she will never succeed. ❞

Racing historian JOHN RANDALL

‘The celebrated Sir Noel Murless (my first mentor in racing) always told me that patience is a trainer’s greatest virtue. This was a lesson confirmed to me by the unparalleled Dr Vincent O’Brien, for whom I was fortunate enough to work in 1977 (and which resulted in my first personal involvement with a Derby winner as I led The Minstrel up to the Derby start and removed the cotton wool from his ears – placed there to muffle the pre-race noise).’

Trainer JOHN GOSDEN unveils the secret of The Minstrel’s Derby success.

John Gosden

❛ The hardest horse I rode was Gyr in the Derby, where we were second to Nijinsky, and in the Grand Prix de Saint-Cloud which I won on the same horse. He was not just wrong in the head but in his mouth. Even when you got off you never stopped riding. By the time you had cantered down to the gate, you'd had enough. The real worry was that so much was expected of him and you didn't have to do much wrong to undo him. I've never been so tired as when I came home after winning the Grand Prix de Saint-Cloud. It was like riding two horses. ❜

Jockey BILL WILLIAMSON, 1974.

Landmarks and Legends 1857

THE FILLY BLINK BONNY WINS THE DERBY AND FORTY-EIGHT HOURS LATER WINS THE OAKS, EMULATING THE FEAT OF ELEANOR IN 1801.

❛ I reckon that it takes at least three hundred horses with breeding to win the Derbv to produce one which is actually capable of winning it. ❜

PETER BURRELL, Director of the National Stud.

‘Just before the Derby Eleanor’s trainer, Cox, was suddenly stricken with a mortal illness. A parson was summoned and the dying man indicated that he wished to impart one final message. The parson duly bent his head to receive it: ‘Depend on it, that Eleanor is the hell of a mare,’ croaked cox, and fell back dead.’

Historian ROGER MORTIMER providing a remarkable insight into Sir Charles Bunbury’s 1801 Derby winner Eleanor.

Eleanor, Eleanor? Are you calling for your wife?

‘My own ambition is to get a Derby winner for the Queen and breed one for myself as well. I hope they don’t come the same year.’

THE EARL OF CARNARVON, the Queen’s racing manager, 1983.

❛ Amato never ran again after his 1838 Derby victory, and eventually was buried at The Durdans. One of the local inns had its name altered to 'The Amato' and a legend was nurtured that at dawn on each Derby Day the name of the winner would be chalked up on the side of a well outside the inn. ❜

Derby historian MICHAEL SETH-SMITH.

Landmarks and Legends 1859

MUSJID'S OWNER SIR JOSEPH HAWLEY CELEBRATES RECORD BACK-TO-BACK DERBY VICTORIES, HAVING WON THE PREVIOUS YEAR'S RUNNING WITH HIS HOME-BRED BEADSMAN.

❛ Stable lads could be bought. In 1825 Middleton started [the Derby] with a bucket of water and a sponge in his stomach, but the people who bribed the lad were unlucky: Middleton still won. ❜

Author and broadcaster ALASTAIR BURNET.

❛ After Pat Eddery had given Golden Fleece a three-furlong spin on the course early on the morning of the race, he came back to report he had coughed three times. After consulting our vet, Bob Griffin, on the phone in Ireland, we decided to take a chance and run him, thinking it might have been the very warm weather that had caused some dryness in his throat. As it turned out, it is certain that he did have a virus when he ran, and that was why he took so long to get over it. ❜

Legendary Irish trainer VINCENT O'BRIEN on 1982 winner Golden Fleece.

'– he had a virus'

❛ I never did think that Shady Heights could win the Derby. It's owned by some bloke from Hong Kong. People like that don't win the Derby. ❜

Chester racegoer, quoted by CHRISTOPHER POOLE, 1987.

‘Nearula should have won the Derby [in 1953]. It was the press who stopped him. While he was being plated before the race, some photographers whom I had allowed into the yard asked the blacksmith to pose. He looked up and pricked Nearula. You can't win a Derby with a lame horse.’

Trainer CAPTAIN CHARLES ELSEY, 1981.

'He pricked Nearula'

‘When Mr Asquith picked out Spion Kop as the winner of the [1920] Derby, he did so because he went about the business of selection not with a pin or a pencil, but with one of the best brains in England. In the course of his long conflicts with the House of Lords he had probably interested himself profoundly in questions of heredity and pedigree, and he was thus well equipped for an investigation into the records of the parentage and grand-parentage of the various Derby horses. ’

NEW STATESMAN, 1920.

‘ So much contributes to breeding a Derby winner and yet, if you try and study it to establish a pattern, all you realize is that there really is none. ’

MARCHIONESS OF TAVISTOCK, 1993.

Landmarks and Legends 1862

CONDITIONS OF THE DERBY ARE ALTERED, WITH THE WEIGHTS FOR COLTS RAISED TO 8ST 10LB AND FILLIES 8ST 5LB, AN INCREASE OF 3LB IN BOTH CASES.

‘ Shirley Heights was a big lazy horse, and at Epsom he didn’t come down the hill. Down the straight, though, he flew and half a furlong from home I thought I was going to win. I suppose in many ways I was lucky because Bill Shoemaker's horse Hawaiian Sound came off the rail just in time. If he hadn't, I would have been in trouble as my horse was lugging down to the rail because of the camber and there would have been no way I could have pulled him around Hawaiian Sound.

Jockey GREVILLE STARKEY grabbed a slice of luck to win the 1978 Derby on Shirley Heights.

Landmarks and Legends 1863

THERE ARE 34 FALSE STARTS BEFORE THE DERBY GETS UNDER WAY.

Blood will tell! – an aphorism as trite as it is true; and, although its truth is daily manifested in horse racing generally, yet in nothing is it more stringently exemplified than in the Derby, in which the best bred and the best trained horses of the day, be they home reared or foreign, compete for the 'blue riband of the Turf.'

THE TIMES, 1873, demonstrating that even then winning the Derby was the ultimate bloodstock and breeding achievement.

A Derby without incident would be a Derby without precedent. If a favourite does not actually break down, goes amiss, meets with an accident or some other misfortune to which racing flesh is heir.

THE TIMES, 1875.

The Derby of 1793 was perhaps the most important one since its foundation, both Waxy, who won, and Gohanna, who was second, being horses of outstanding merit. Both, moreover. and in particular Waxy, have left their mark in the Stud Book.

Historian ROGER MORTIMER underlining that even in the earliest days of the race the true value of a Derby winner was at stud.

Did you leave this in Waxy's box? Well he's been and gone and left his mark on it!

Sceptre is Persimmon's daughter
She's trained on the Wiltshire Downs.
Wednesday's the day she ought to
Fill Bob Sievier's pockets with pounds!

Variety artist GERTIE MILLER's variation to the chorus of 'The Miller's Daughter', sung to the occupants of owner–trainer Bob Sievier's box at the Gaiety Theatre the night before the 1902 Derby. The confidence was, alas, misplaced, although Sceptre did win the Oaks two days later.

In this year [1784] there were signs that the Derby was already regarded as a race of some consequence, for in the Sion Sweepstakes at Newmarket in October, winners of the Cumberland or Derby Stakes were required to carry six pounds extra.

Historian ROGER MORTIMER providing evidence that within four years of its inauguration the Derby was already a race of some status.

Landmarks and Legends 1865

GLADIATEUR, OWNED BY THE SON OF ONE OF NAPOLEON'S GENERALS, IS THE FIRST FRENCH-BRED WINNER OF THE RACE.

If you want the best, you breed the best to the best, and hope for the best.

COLONEL EDWARD BRADLEY lists the ingredients required to breed a Derby winner.

Landmarks and Legends 1866

LORD LYON AT ODDS OF 5-6, BECOMES THE FIRST ODDS-ON FAVOURITE TO WIN THE DERBY FOR 74 YEARS.

Everyone who is thrilled by the Derby should walk the course at Epsom just once. It is an amazing experience.

MARCHIONESS OF TAVISTOCK, 1993.

Of course, there was no shortage of disparaging critics to say that in order to have won as he did [from eighth and boxed in at two-furlongs out to win by seven lengths], Troy must have been facing exceptionally mediocre opponents. As a matter of fact, [among those he beat], Dickens Hill won the

Coral Eclipse Stakes; Northern Baby the Champion Stakes; Ela-Mana-Mou won the King Edward VII Stakes and the following year the Eclipse Stakes and King George VI and Queen Elizabeth Diamond Stakes; Milford won the Princess of Wales's Stakes; Niniski won the Geoffrey Freer Stakes, the Irish St Leger and the Prix-Royal Oak; and Son Of Love won the St Leger, in which Niniski was third. ❜

Racing historian ROGER MORTIMER in no doubt as to the brilliance of Troy's victory in the 1979 Derby.

Landmarks and Legends 1868

HIS HEART SET ON OWNING A DERBY WINNER, ARCHIBALD PRIMROSE, FUTURE FIFTH EARL OF ROSEBERY, DROPS OUT OF CHRIST CHURCH, OXFORD, AFTER THE AUTHORITIES THERE TELL HIM, 'EITHER THE HORSE GOES OR YOU DO . . . '

❛ There is probably no course in England so likely to find out the weak points in a candidate under suspicion in regard to respiratory organs as the ups and downs of the Surrey hills, to compass which successfully has always been considered the crucial test of a horse's soundness. ’

THE TIMES, 1879, on the testing nature of the Derby course.

Landmarks and Legends 1872

THE PRESENT DERBY COURSE IS FIRST USED.

‘ If ever there was a racecourse with idiosyncrasies equipped to give excuses for beaten racehorses, Epsom is surely it. ’

Racing historian ROGER MORTIMER.

‘ The Derby now has a weaker grip on the firmament, but for the traditionalists and participants, it remains *the* contest, the examination which defines the racing horse. ’

Journalist RICHARD EDMONDSON.

❛ The [Derby] course was as hard and grassless as a GLC playground; the little grey just skittered along. ❜

Racing historian ROGER MORTIMER writing about Mahmoud's then record time in the 1936 Derby.

❛ It has always been a mystery to me why our best race should be run on our worst racecourse. ❜

BBC television racing presenter JULIAN WILSON

Julian Wilson

"The Derby is won and lost on the climb up the hill during the first half mile. If you go up the hill using petrol to get a position, you will be in trouble."

Triple Derby-winning jockey WALTER SWINBURN.

Landmarks and Legends 1877

SILVIO PROVIDES JOCKEY FRED ARCHER WITH THE FIRST OF HIS FOUR DERBY VICTORIES.

"*Flushed red are American faces!*
Hurrah! for old Leamington's son.
You'll show the pale Briton how races
Across the Atlantic are run.
Dash on as if life was at Venture
And news shall unloosen the cork
From seas of champagne at Newmarket
And oceans of 'fizz' in New York!"

Ditty composed in honour of America's first Derby winner Iroquois, 1881

❝ Epsom week is our Olympic Games. ❞

LORD PALMERSTON, 1847.

❝ I felt every moment that I was going to be shot over his head, his propelling power is so terrific. ❞

Ormonde's owner THE DUKE OF WESTMINSTER, an accomplished horseman, describing the sensation of riding the 1886 Derby winne

Landmarks and Legends 1879

SIR BEVYS WINS THE DERBY. STRUCK BY THE ARTHURIAN NAME, THE POET LAUREATE ALFRED TENNYSON COLLECTS £100 FROM A £5 BET.

❝ The greatest Flat champion of the twentieth century, French ace Sea Bird won seven of his eight races and achieved legendary status with his awesome victories in the Derby and Prix de l'Arc de Triomphe in 1965. At Epsom the Etienne Pollet-trained favourite won without coming off the bridle, cantering to the front over a furlong from home and just being pushed out by Pat

Glennon for 100 yards before being eased. The top-class runner-up, Meadow Court, was flattered by the two-length margin. ❞

Racing journalist and historian JOHN RANDALL in no doubt as to the identity of the greatest Derby winner of all.

Landmarks and Legends 1881

IROQUOIS BECOMES THE FIRST AMERICAN-BRED DERBY WINNER.

❝ It is the championship for three-year-olds. If you look back at the records you can see that whatever wins the Derby has to be a great horse. He has to have the speed to get out of trouble, but he must also stay one and a half miles. He has to be able to run uphill, downhill, and keep well balanced round Tattenham Corner. He must possess all the qualities that make him a great horse. ❞

Jockey FRANKIE DETTORI, 1996.

❝ Humorist's victory in the 1921 Derby was gained by a colt whose courage knew no bounds, and who was dead a fortnight after his glorious Epsom triumph. His dramatic and tragic death, caused by a tubercular lung condition, had not been detected when he contested the Derby, and in the circumstances his heroic gallantry was nothing short of miraculous. ❜

Racing historian MICHAEL SETH-SMITH extolling Humorist's remarkable achievement in winning the 1921 Derby.

Landmarks and Legends 1882

THE DERBY AND EACH OF THE OTHER FOUR CLASSIC RACES ARE WON BY FILLIES.

❛ I have seen all the best horse that have flourished and had their day for more than sixty years past, and I now repeat my well considered opinion that Priam was the most perfect racehorse I ever saw. His constitution was magnificently sound; his temperament and nervous system beautifully attuned; his shape, make, and action were faultless. ❜

Jockey JOHN KENT Jr expounding the virtues of Priam, the 1830 Derby winner.

And if, of the outsiders there,
Just one should pass the winning chair,
Enrolled in the successful three,
Be sure Caractacus is he.

Tipster in *BELL'S LIFE* getting it absolutely spot on – Caractacus won the 1862 Derby at the odds of 40-1.

Landmarks and Legends 1884

ST GATIEN AND HARVESTER RUN THE SECOND DEAD HEAT IN DERBY HISTORY BUT UNLIKE IN 1828, THE STAKES ARE DIVIDED.

In short, if you'd summer in clover
And send to the devil the Jews
Believe me, the Derby is over
Blair Athol can't possibly lose!

An anonymous tipster in the run-up to the 1864 Derby won by Blair Athol.

' Our French neighbours are difficult to beat at any game. By clever investments they have secured our best blood. Look to your laurels, gentlemen! They have gone 'bang up your heads'. '

ADMIRAL ROUS's rallying cry following the victory of the French-bred colt Gladiateur in the 1865 Derby.

Landmarks and Legends **1888**

PRIZE MONEY FOR THE DERBY FALLS BELOW £4,000 FOR THE FIRST TIME IN ALMOST HALF A CENTURY.

' For one second only, I thought this is it. When I went passed Fahal I glanced up to see how far we were from home. As soon as the winning post came into sight I saw Walter [Swinburn] and Lammtarra coming. But for a mini-second I still believed the dream was about to come true. '

Jockey FRANKIE DETTORI, rider of runner-up Tamure in the 1995 Derby.

Landmarks and Legends 1890

CONDITIONS OF THE DERBY CHANGED FROM BEING A £50 SWEEPSTAKES TO A RACE WITH A GUARANTEED VALUE OF £5,000.

“I could not believe the Epsom track when I first saw it. My first ride was in 1991 and it was then that I realised how unusual it is. It is so difficult for the horses, but that is why whatever wins the Derby is the best horse because he has to have every quality.”

Jockey FRANKIE DETTORI, 1996.

“They all get excited about the Arc, the Breeders' Cup and the Dubai World Cup, but the Epsom Derby will always be number one in my book. The unique gradients of the course mean that a horse has to be able to lead on both legs, hold a stride and possess a perfect blend of speed and stamina. Where else do you have to cross two roads during a race?”

Former jockey JIMMY LINDLEY detailing the requirements needed to win a Derby.

People talk about Epsom being an easy mile and a half, but that is nonsense – non-stayers don't win the Derby.

Former jockey JIMMY LINDLEY, 1996.

There was some disappointment when the colt [Generous] could finish no closer than fourth in the 2,000 Guineas. But there is an old saying in racing - fourth in the Guineas, first in the Derby.

Racing journalist COLIN MACKENZIE, 2000.

Landmarks and Legends **1894**

THE PRIME MINISTER ARCHIBALD PRIMROSE, FIFTH EARL OF ROSEBERY, WINS WITH LADAS, A FEAT EMULATED BY THE SAME OWNER'S SIR VISTO THE FOLLOWING YEAR.

If you look at it sensibly, and the Derby hadn't always been here, you'd probably never run a race at Epsom at all.

Former Epsom Managing Director TIM NELIGAN, 1993.

The line between a top Derby distance twelve-furlong horse and a slow plodder, with no commercial salvage value, is so thin as to be indefinable.

Journalist JULIAN MUSCAT, 1997.

More than one expert, such as the BBC's racing correspondent Julian Wilson, has insisted that the Derby should be held somewhere else, but that would be unthinkable. For it is the sheer eccentricity of Epsom that makes the English Derby a unique test of a racehorse.

Author and broadcaster ALASTAIR BURNET, 1993.

Landmarks and Legends 1895

THE DERBY IS THE FIRST HORSE RACE TO BE FILMED.

Derby winners come from dedication, determination and sheer luck.

ALASTAIR BURNET.

FIVE

The World's Greatest Race

A Time-Honoured Tradition

> The Derby is the most famous event in the world's racing calendar and I send my very best wishes for a very successful bicentenary. I shall look forward to being present again.

Letter from HER MAJESTY THE QUEEN to the Chairman of United Racecourses in May 1979, prior to the 200th running of the Derby.

> The Derby is not only the greatest and most prestigious horse-race in the world, it is a British institution with a hold on the public well beyond the world of racing.

ALASTAIR BURNET, 1993.

❛ With a substantial number of stories, some romantic, some eccentric, some scurrilous, many surprising, attached to the history of the Derby and those involved in it, it is no easy task selecting a few of the most memorable runnings as a means of hinting at the race's rich flavour, this even if the period under consideration is restricted to the twentieth century. ❜

TIMEFORM NEWS, 1983.

❛ No one present had any conception of the historic importance of the occasion, and the Derby was considered no more than an incidental contest which was included in the afternoon's sporting programme to decide which of the subscribers' thoroughbreds was the best three-year-old miler. ❜

Writer and BBC radio racing commentator MICHAEL SETH-SMITH recalling the inaugural running of the Derby in 1780.

❛ The fact that the word 'Derby' signifies the supreme race in many countries around the world can mean only one thing – that the Epsom Derby was at the beginning and always has been the touchstone of the champion. ❜

American PAUL MELLON, owner of the 1971 Derby winner Mill Reef.

'There is no winning post that stands besides Epsom's in the world.'

ALASTAIR BURNET, 1993.

'The Derby at Epsom is purely and simply the greatest horse race in the world! Some people may find that statement contentious yet you won't find many breeders in the world who would pick any other race of which they would rather breed the winner. There are many races in other countries that are more valuable in terms of prize money, that are certainly run on a more sensible race track, but I do not believe that any other race is as emotive or charismatic.'

MARCHIONESS OF TAVISTOCK, 1993.

Landmarks and Legends 1896

PERSIMMON WINS THE DERBY FOR THE PRINCE OF WALES.

'Anyone who does not consider the Epsom Derby one of the greatest sporting events in the world must be out of his mind.'

JOHN GALBREATH, owner of 1972 Derby winner Roberto.

‘Epsom is the place you must like before all others.’

JOSS TOLAND, 1711.

‘The Derby is a little like your first experience of sex – hectic, strenuous, memorably pleasant and over before you know it.’

American writer BILL BRYSON, 1990.

– Is that it then?

‘Almost everything to do with the naming of the Derby is surmised and one can only suppose that the success of the Oaks, first run in 1779, and the fact that my ancestor, the 12th Earl of Derby, had won the race, inspired him to think of greater things. However, it does seem fairly clear that the Derby was conceived at a dinner party at 'The Oaks' at which Sir Charles Bunbury was present. Some doubt is thrown on the story that he and Sir Charles tossed up to decide whether the race should be called the 'Derby' or the 'Bunbury'. My grandfather always maintained that the story was true. ❞

THE 14TH EARL OF DERBY, 1979.

❝ And as a spectacle, for it certainly is one, the scene at Epsom on Derbv Day is the finest of all spectacles in the calendar. ❞

Leader in *THE TIMES*, 1921.

That's nothing! You should go to Epsom on Derby Day!

❛ Derby Day is something special. There's a higher degree of tension among the riders. It's the greatest day's racing in the English calendar for the people – you just can't move. ❜

Nine times Derby-winning jockey LESTER PIGGOTT.

Landmarks and Legends 1899

THE DERBY IS STARTED BY FLAG FOR THE LAST TIME

❛ Sponsored or unsponsored, may it [the Derby] continue for ever, for surely it has been sponsored by heaven from the beginning. ❜

PAUL MELLON, owner of 1971 Derby winner Mill Reef..

❛ Only when the Derby field is at the post, and the start of the race is nigh, does the gaiety of the crowd begin to change. The shout 'They're off!' and then just for a moment the penetrating silence of half a million comes over the downs, the dash of colour up the hill, the desperate descent to Tattenham

Corner, and then the long, agonising struggle in the short straight – the most exciting half-minute of the racing year.

Racing historian BILL CURLING, 1951.

Landmarks and Legends 1900

THE STARTING GATE IS USED FOR THE FIRST TIME.

❛ Such is the prestige, such is the magic of the Derby Day, a prestige and a magic which neither the disabilities of the railways can depress nor the fascination of golf outrival. ❜

THE TIMES, 1921.

❛ There was certainly no point in the history of racing or breeding at which somebody said, 'Now let's think out the ideal race in terms of distance and course and call it this or that,' and came up with the idea of one and a half miles at Epsom. ❜

PETER BURRELL, Director of the National Stud.

‘This might be the most famous race in the world, but it appeals to people who’ve no interest in sport.’

Journalist ANTHONY CLAVANE.

‘A roistering party at a country house founded two races, and named them gratefully after their host and his house, the Derby and the Oaks. Seldom has a carouse had a more permanent effect.’

LORD ROSEBERY, questioning the legend that the name of the Derby was decided on the toss of a coin.

Landmarks and Legends 1903

DANNY MAHER BECOMES THE THIRD AMERICAN RIDER IN SUCCESSION TO WIN THE DERBY WHEN SCORING ON ROCK SAND. GUARANTEED VALUE IS INCREASED TO £6,500.

‘Among the alterations and improvements that have been made for facilitating the business of the meeting, nothing more important has been effected than that extension of telegraph wires from Croydon to the Grand Stand on Epsom Downs. Until the present meeting expresses have been ordinarily transmitted by pigeons, a mode that was not without its inconveniences, but which will now be wholly obviated, by the rapidity, certainty and the illimitable use that may be made of the wires as a means of communication. ❞

Report in *THE TIMES*, 1853.

❝ The Derby being a Classic race, it is felt that the winner must have at least a not quite undignified name, and from this feeling arises the doctrine of the winning name. Sansovino, Blenheim and Hyperion, for example, would be given a very good chance on this method of selection, and believers in this doctrine would at once rule out of consideration Sponge Bun or Cabbage Patch on the ground of the vulgarity of their names. ❞

GUY GRIFFITH and MICHAEL OAKSHOTT in
A Guide to the Classics, 1936.

❝ God knows, you've got no chance with a race like the Derby. The bastards are all trying. ❞

A head lad to writer JEFFREY BERNARD, 1979.

❛ In the first place you don't see it and in the second – to be Irish on the occasion of a frolic – you perceive it to be not much worth seeing . . . a dozen furiously revolving arms – pink, green, orange, scarlet, white – whacking the flanks of as many straining steeds; a glimpse of this and the spectacle is over. The spectacle however is of course an infinitesimally small part of the purpose of Epsom and the interest in the Derby. ❜

Having travelled to the Derby on the top of an omnibus in the 1870's, American novelist HENRY JAMES was unimpressed by the race.

Landmarks and Legends 1905

CICERO SETS A NEW RECORD TIME FOR THE DERBY OF 2 MINUTES 39 2/5 SECONDS.

❛ I can't stress too much what a tiny arrow-slit of opportunity the Derby is – you get one shot, round a Disney ride of a racecourse, with a pubescent horse who is still learning the trade. ❜

Journalist and television broadcaster ALASTAIR DOWN.

'The Derby is Britain's biggest day out.'

STEPHEN WALLIS, Managing Director of Epsom Downs Racecourse.

'My funniest recollection of the Derby, though, was back in 1931. I'd chosen Cameronian and backed my judgement. On Derby Day a salesman brought a new Hoover to demonstrate to my wife. Eileen told him: 'If Cameronian wins I'll have it. If it doesn't you can take it away.' So there they were sitting by the radio both shouting like mad for Cameronian. The chap wasn't a racing man but I bet he never forgot Cameronian making that sale for him.'

Journalist TOM E. WEBSTER, 1975.

'Come on Cameronian, then we can both "clean up"!'

Let no man who has no need, who is not in danger of losing all he has, and is not obliged to grasp at every chance, make a book on the Derby. While the fever it excites is raging, and the odds are varying, I can neither read nor write nor occupy myself with anything else.

Diarist CHARLES GREVILLE, 1833.

Landmarks and Legends 1906

SPEARMINT BEATS CICERO'S RECORD TIME, CLOCKING 2 MINUTES 36 4/5 SECONDS.

The Derby is the Blue Riband of the Turf.

BENJAMIN DISRAELI, 1848, in his *Life of George Bentinck.*

A panic in the stock market, when companies are crumbling, and the funds falling two, three and four per cent in the hour, and foreign shares are dwindling away next to nothing, when each haggard messenger brings tidings of a rise in the bank rate, and the discount houses won't touch legitimate paper and good bills at short dates under an unprecedented price – when every telegram brings fresh reports of monetary convulsions in every capital in Europe, and men look terror-stricken at one another, and blanch with a nameless dread of some unheard-of catastrophe – is as nothing to the race for the Derby. ❜

THE DERBY DAY – A SPORTING NOVEL, 1864.

Landmarks and Legends **1907**

ORBY IS THE FIRST IRISH-TRAINED WINNER.

❛ The Derby Day puts us in mind of our national theatres on the first night of pantomime. ❜

A cynical view in *THE TIMES*, 1842.

❛ The road to Epsom was crowded with all descriptions of people hurtling to the races; some to plunder and some to be plundered. Horses, gigs, curricles, coaches, chaises, carts and pedestrians covered with dust crowded the

Downs, the peoɒle running and jostling each other as they made contact. ❜

THE TIMES, 1793.

❛ There is no such race as the Epsom Derby. What's run at Epsom is *the* Derby; its imitators are the ones that require geographical qualifiers. ❜

Journalist PAUL HAIGH.

Landmarks and Legends 1908

SIGNORINETTA WINS THE DERBY AT ODDS OF 100-1 AND THE OAKS TWO DAYS LATER.

❛ Everyone hates me and I like it. ❜

Epsom's hugely unpopular and extremely rude Clerk of the Course HENRY MAYSON DORLING, who held the office from 1873 to 1919 and delighted in being known as the 'Dictator of Epsom'.

❛ It is still the race that the professionals most want to win, it still regularly produces champions, and it is still a special occasion for a large section of the community. ❜

Journalists TONY MORRIS and JOHN RANDALL in
A Century of Champions 1999.

Landmarks and Legends 1909

THE VICTORY OF MINORU FOR KING EDWARD VII PROVIDES THE ONLY OCCASION ON WHICH THE DERBY WINNER HAS BEEN OWNED BY THE REIGNING MONARCH.

❛ By one o'clock there must have been eighty thousand persons assembled on the Downs – what they all went thither for is best known to themselves, but certainly not one twentieth of them saw the race, and the only other amusements were broiling on an arid heath beneath a mid-day sun, or sitting in booths crowded to suffocation amidst the fumes of tobacco and all sorts of hideous uproar. ❜

BELL'S LIFE IN LONDON, 1823.

I'm glad to hear you did not scorch your fingers over the Derby. I didn't myself either, but I shall take good care of how I embark on such matters again, and I can't help advising you to do the same. It isn't very satisfactory to win and highly unpleasant to lose.

Letter from EDWARD LYTTELTON to George Nathaniel Curzon, when schoolboys at Eton.

Landmarks and Legends 1913

TWO SENSATIONS. THE SUFFRAGETTE EMILY DAVISON IS FELLED BY KING GEORGE V'S HORSE ANMER AT TATTENHAM CORNER, THEN THE FAVOURITE CRAGANOUR, FIRST PAST THE POST, IS DISQUALIFIED IN FAVOUR OF 100-1 OUTSIDER ABOYEUR.

Epsom is a happy home for the Derby. Geographically it is good, for it is only fifteen miles from Piccadilly Circus, and it is easy of approach from the largest city in the world. As a test of the racehorse it is good, for the winner must be able to go up hill and down dale, and from the spectator's point of view it is good, for the stands are on high ground, and the course and far beyond it can be seen from many angles. ❞

Racing historian BILL CURLING, 1951.

❝ The 'Derby Day' is a sort of era in the lives of most persons, and certain classes are accustomed to date from, or refer events to, the anniversary of its recurrence; so that, independently of its sporting importance, it has a chain as the *terminus a quo or ad quem* by which a portion of the community calculate the revolution of time. ❞

THE TIMES, 1844.

❝ The Derby is still the greatest race in the world, but I do think there have to be some slight changes to it. I've always been a Wednesday person, and I think it needs a move back there. I'm not impressed with where they've put the parade ring either. I've got a chicken that lays an egg as big as that paddock. It's a selfish paddock, not where Joe Bloggs can get a decent view. I'd also like to see the horses doing the Derby walk down to the start again. That was all part of the test of horse and jockey, getting through all those people shouting and the music blaring away. ❞

GEOFF LEWIS, rider of 1971 Derby winner Mill Reef, 1997.

❛ The great English festival is one to which every one comes attired in his holyday feelings and pleasant looks. A man must be of sour, austere character indeed, no ray of sunshine can ever have lost its way into his churlish heart, if he refuses to bear his part in the general mirth today. ❜

Derby Day report in *THE TIMES*, 1860.

❛ To write anything new about the Derby-day as a spectacle we hold to be an impossibility. ❜

THE TIMES, 1878.

❛ *On Epsom Downs when racing does begin,*
Large companies from every part come in,
Tag rag and bob-tail, lords and ladies meet,
And squires without estates each other greet,
A scoundrel here, pray take on my word,
Is a companion for the greatest lord,
Provided that his purse abounds with gold,
If not, then his affection will not hold.
Here the promiscuous and ungovern'd crew
Crowds to see what is neither strange or new:
Bets upon bets, this man says – two to one,
Another pointing cries, Good sir, 'tis done.

See how they gallop o'er the spacious plain,
As if persu'd, and the dreading to be slain;
Not half such speed would any of them make
To save their country if she lay at stake.
The races done, to town the mob repair.
Some curse their fate, and some the booty share.

Anonymous ditty, 1735.

'To town the mob repair'

On no other racing occasion of the year is the cry 'Come Racing!' made more urgently than on Derby Day. The masses thronging the Downs, the top-hatted toffs poncing around in the Club enclosure, the betting ring throbbing with the hectic, urgent final exchanges of one of the biggest betting events of the year – Derby Day has the lot. ❞

Racing journalist and television presenter JOHN MCCRIRICK, 1993.

Landmarks and Legends 1914

DURBAR BECOMES THE FIRST FRENCH-TRAINED HORSE TO WIN THE DERBY.

❝ Epsom itself, still rural and unspoiled, was converted during raceweek into a seething city, doubtless to the great satisfaction and profit of the local shopkeepers who charged famine prices for food. Until the local constabulary was instituted race-week invariably heralded a crime wave, and a contemporary writer observed, 'The viscous and unprincipled form a tolerable proportion of the crowd, and it generally follows that many atrocities are committed.' ❞

Historian ROGER MORTIMER records how in the eighteenth century Epsom during race-week became a breeding ground for crime.

' The pre-eminence of the Derby is an essential mix of tradition, consistency and innovation. '

SIR EVELYN DE ROTHSCHILD, 1993.

Landmarks and Legends **1915**

BECAUSE OF THE WAR, THE DERBY IS TRANSFERRED FROM EPSOM TO THE JULY COURSE AT NEWMARKET, WHERE IT IS RUN UNTIL RETURNING TO EPSOM IN 1919.

' The Derby has attracted ante-post legends, most famously owner Raymond Guest backing one of his two-year-olds for the 1968 race at 100-1 with William Hill. When it came to naming the colt, Guest called it Sir Ivor, and it took only a ride of genius from Lester Piggott to bring the Vincent O'Brien champion home in the Derby at 'wrist on' [4-5]. '

Channel 4 Racing betting guru JOHN MCCRIRICK, 1993.

' My first visit to Epsom was in the May of 1856 – Blink Bonny's year. My first Derby had no interest for me as a race, but as giving me the opportunity of studying life and character, it is ever to be gratefully remembered. ❞

Artist WILLIAM POWELL FRITH, whose recollections are not as clear as his narrative painting *Derby Day*, as Ellington won the Derby in 1856. Blink Bonny's year was 1857.

Landmarks and Legends 1917

THE DERBY IS NOT RUN UNTIL 31 JULY AFTER PARLIAMENT HAS SUSPENDED RACING EARLIER IN THE YEAR DUE TO LACK OF RESOURCES BROUGHT ON BY THE WAR.

❝ Epsom Downs on Derby Day is the most astonishing, the most varied, the most glorious spectacle that ever was, or ever can be, under any circumstances, visible to the mortal eye. ❞

ILLUSTRATED LONDON NEWS

Landmarks and Legends 1918

LADY JAMES DOUGLAS BECOMES THE FIRST WOMAN OWNER TO WIN THE DERBY WHEN GAINSBOROUGH LANDS THE WAR-TIME SUBSTITUTE RACE AT NEWMARKET.

SIX

A Day on the Downs

The Derby Experience

“The highway to Epsom was covered with vehicles of every description between and beyond adennes and a dog-cart. Travelling necessarily became slow and dangerous. The venturesome and impatient continually broke through the line, and produced the greatest confusion. Traces were broken, panels driven in, chaises overturned, shafts shattered, and toll-bars defied and dislocated. In fact, from Kensington Gate to the race-course there was but one unbroken line of dust, din and disturbance.”

Mayhem on the road to Epsom, *THE TIMES*, 1837.

“A few minutes, only a few minutes, and the event that for twelve months has been the pivot of so much calculation, of such subtle combinations, of such deep conspiracies, round which the thought and passion of the sporting world have hung like eagles, will be recorded in the fleeting tablets of the past. But what minutes! Count them by sensation, and each moment is a day and the race a life. ”

BENJAMIN DISRAELI, *Sybil*, 1845.

“ Last year it was iced champagne, claret cup and silk overcoats; now it out to be hot brandy and water, foot baths and flannels. ”

CHARLES DICKENS describing the 1863 Derby, which was run on an appallingly wet day.

A day of extraordinary excitement and interest to the sportsman, and to millions of others in every part of England, from the manufacturers of twelve stories high to the Yorkshire ploughman; from the cockney behind his counter to the cellarman at Hatchett's.

BEN MARSHALL, painter and journalist, describing Derby Day in 1830.

'I've entered 'im for the Derby – 'e pulls the plough faster than the 'oss I backed last year!'

There is a full hour to go now between the Diomed and the Derby itself. The funfair crowds are getting larger and more abandoned and the sense of delicious and delayed anticipation seems to rise and reverberate with the amplified sound of the music.

Author JAMIE REID, 1988.

❛ The trend for gypsies to converge on Epsom during Derby week is almost as old as the Derby itself and they feature in numerous historic paintings of what used to be an even bigger occasion than it is today. The gypsies, attracted by the crowds, became a fixture, although the track management has not always welcomed their presence. ❜

Racing journalist SEB VANCE.

Landmarks and Legends 1919

THE DERBY RETURNS TO EPSOM AFTER ITS EVACUATION TO NEWMARKET DURING WORLD WAR I AND IS POPULARLY KNOWN AS THE PEACE DERBY.

❛ Cockney carnival and suburban saturnalia. ❜

SIR WILFRED LAWSON describing the 1875 Derby.

❛ That Miss Emily Wilding Davison died of a fracture of the base of the skull, caused by being accidentally knocked down by a horse through wilfully rushing onto the racecourse at

Epsom Downs during the progress of the race for the Derby: death was due to misadventure.

Findings of coroner at the inquest of the suffragette who lost her life when she brought the King's horse Anmer down in the 1913 Derby.

Landmarks and Legends 1922

CAPTAIN CUTTLE BECOMES THE FIRST OF TRAINER FRED DARLING'S SEVEN DERBY WINNERS, SETTING A NEW COURSE RECORD OF 2 MINUTES 34 3/5 SECS.

The town of Epsom was packed to capacity with accommodation almost impossible to procure, and one gentlemen who wished to procure a house for race-week was asked for the equivalent of two years rent.

Writer and BBC radio racing commentator MICHAEL SETH-SMITH highlighting the cost of accommodation in Epsom for the 1788 Derby.

At an early hour London, like a huge leviathan, poured forth its thousands for this metropolitan jubilee, and the country for miles around contributed its quota to swell the crowd. The road, as usual, was one of splendid confusion, and there were the customary delays, squabbles, and mishaps. ❜

Derby day report in *THE TIMES*, 1828.

Wait 'till these railways they've just invented get going – then you really will see delays!

❛ 'The laws of the road on Derby Day': To stand up in your carriage, to shout, to use your arms like a wild telegraph, and your legs like a pair of mad compasses, to talk, joke and laugh in the easiest and decidedly freest manner, with persons you would be ashamed of being seen to exchange a single word with on any other occasion but the Derby.

PUNCH, 1859.

Landmarks and Legends **1924**

SANSOVINO PROVIDES THE STANLEY FAMILY WITH ITS FIRST WINNER SINCE SIR PETER TEAZLE WON FOR THE EARL OF DERBY IN 1787.

Hearty, jovial, social equality are the order of the day; and for once the short pipe and the regalia are brethren, and the penny Pickwick is quite as good as the Laferme cigarette. Nobody puts on 'side' or assumes superior attitudes. If he did he would be chaffed, as the saying is, into or out of his boots.

GEORGE AUGUSTUS SALA, 1892.

No fantasy is more unlikely, or more probable, than the Derby, a race which is perpetual, unmatched, immortal.

Author and broadcaster ALASTAIR BURNET.

❛ Any fool can make money on a Derby Day. In fact, they throw it at you. ❜

A tipster at the Derby in the early twentieth century.

– They throw it at you!

❛ The most curious spectacle is the human tide which, instantaneously and in a body, pours forth and rolls over the course behind the runners, like a wave of ink: the black and motionless crowd has suddenly melted and become molten; in a moment it spreads itself abroad in vast proportions till the eye cannot follow it. ❜

Frenchman HIPPOLYTE TAINE, visiting the Derby in 1870.

❛ It [Derby Day] gives all London an airing. ❜

French artist GUSTAVE DORÉ, 1872.

Landmarks and Legends **1923**

STEVE DONOGHUE BECOMES THE FIRST AND ONLY JOCKEY TO WIN THREE SUCCESSIVE DERBYS.

❛ In the principal stand were assembled almost all the whole of the sporting aristocracy of the country; the extraordinary display of female beauty and the elegant dresses of the ladies, gave it almost a resemblance to a scene of fairy land and has the most joyous and delightful appearance. ❜

THE TIMES, 1836.

❛ I see nothing noble or manly about it. What is there manly in going and sitting on a stand, in a cloud of dust, surrounded by a crowd of bawling blacklegs [bookmakers] - sitting there watching twenty jockeys making twenty horses gallop as fast as they can? ❜

A dissenting view from SIR WILFRED LAWSON, 1880.

Landmarks and Legends 1927

THE DERBY IS BROADCAST ON RADIO BY THE BBC FOR THE FIRST TIME.

'I like a horse! nay, more I like the Races!
Yes, have a flare-up and enjoy the fun.
But most of all, admire the pretty faces
At splendid Epsom, with its glorious run!
I like to see the Four! the Swells! the Graces!
And those 'would-be' wits, so inclined to pun:
The company lively, jolly, merry, gay,
Pleased with the ride, the races and the play.'

Satirical commentator PIERCE EGAN, 1835.

Landmarks and Legends 1930

BLENHEIM PROVIDES THE AGA KHAN WITH HIS FIRST WINNER OF THE DERBY. IT IS THE FIRST YEAR THAT TOTALISATOR IS OPERATED ON THE DERBY.

'They do not swarm to Epsom like they used to, of course. But then, when it was in midweek, it was perceived as the annual skive, the great Londoners' day out; rarely have so many grandmothers been buried on the first Wednesday in June.'

Journalist NICK TOWNSEND.

Sorry sir – we just cannot cope with any more Grandmothers!

'The guests of 'Gordy' White (created a life peer in 1991 by Mrs Thatcher) have added lustre for the rubberneckers who treat the Derby not so much as a race but a day out, mixing with a full cross-section of British society, from princes to paupers, dukes to didicoys. ❜

Diarist NIGEL DEMPSTER, 1993.

Landmarks and Legends 1932

THE DERBY IS THE FIRST RACE TO BE TELEVISED.

❛ I could not imagine that anyone with a sense of Englishness would not want to go to the Derby. I could not imagine that anyone with a feel for sport would not find, in the Derby, one of the year's most perfect moments. In the great crowd and the great race I found. not a single entity, but separate forces of comparable power. ❜

Journalist LAURA THOMPSON (1996) recalling her first visit to the Derby in 1991.

❛ Yesterday was the great and eventful day at this place, the 'Derby' day, a name which enlivens every inhabitant of the neighbourhood within fifty miles of it. Every Derby for the last twenty years, providing the weather has been favourable, has been said to be more numerously attended than any that have preceded it. ❞

The ever-increasing popularity of Derby Day, underlined by *THE TIMES*, 1836.

Landmarks and Legends 1937

MRS LETTICE MILLER BECOMES THE FIRST LADY TO OWN AN EPSOM DERBY WINNER WITH MID-DAY SUN.

❝ On Derby Day the patrician puts his pride into the pocket of his gossamer paletot [loose garment] and is perfectly ready to be hail fellow well met with the humblest of the working classes. None save the most ill-conditioned curmudgeons lose their temper at the witticisms levelled at them on the Hill or in coming and going. If things are thrown at you, just throw them back. But there are limits – oranges and lobster claws are just all right but not bags of flour and bad eggs. ❞

Mid-nineteenth century observations in the *ILLUSTRATED LONDON NEWS.*

‘In its early years the Derby was witnessed by a mere five thousand or so spectators; by the 1850s the number had risen to sixty thousand, and by the twentieth century to a quarter of a million.’

Historian ROGER MORTIMER outlining the Derby's growth in terms of attendances.

‘On the Derby morning, all London wakes at cockcrow. The first flicker of light breaks upon thousands of busy men in misty stables ... breaks upon lines of loaded pedestrians footing it from London, to turn a penny at the great event.’

BLANCHARD JERROLD, 1872.

'Busy men in misty stables'

'To me it is a matter of perfect indifference whether the House adjourns or not. To the Derby I will go. I have not missed that event for thirty years, and I am not going to miss it at my present advanced period of life.'

JOHN WILLIAM MACLURE, MP, joining the debate in the 1890s calling for the abolition of the tradition of the House of Commons to adjourn so that Members could go to the Derby.

Landmarks and Legends 1940

THE DERBY IS AGAIN MOVED TO THE JULY COURSE AT NEWMARKET ON ACCOUNT OF WAR.

'On Epsom downs excitement was pent up and crowds flocked to booths to see the girl described as 'The Champion High Kicker', the African and Zulu Exhibition and the young midget boxer who weighed only 3st 4lb. There were dwarfs, clowns, acrobats and a fun-fair with merry-go-round and swings, 'nigger minstrels', tipsters, pick-pockets, card-sharps and sellers of ginger beer all adding to the hustle and bustle, the noise and the hubbub of the occasion.'

Racing historian MICHAEL SETH-SMITH describing the scene on Derby Day 1896.

❛ Preparing for the Derby is an elaborate affair. The lucky tie and the winning suit must be worn; a sharp eye must be kept for black cats and chimney sweeps; an inner significance must be looked for in every incident of the journey. It is scarcely to be wondered at that going to the Derby is about the most tiring holiday a man may take, as well as the pleasantest. ❜

GUY GRIFFITH and MICHAEL OAKSHOTT,
A Guide to the Classics 1936.

'But it's my lucky tie and winning suit! – Don't you remember, I wore it the day we met'

Landmarks and Legends **1941**

OWEN TUDOR PROVIDES LEGENDARY TRAINER FRED DARLING WITH HIS SEVENTH AND FINAL SUCCESS IN THE DERBY.

❛ Peers and plebs alike were unrestrained in their enthusiasm. Silk hats and flat caps consigned to the air in careless rapture. It was the most frenetic display of communal delirium racing has ever inspired. ❜

The scene after Persimmon's 1896 victory, described in *Great Moments in Racing.*

❛ In the first week of June, Epsom is the only place to be – and be seen to be. ❜

Diarist NIGEL DEMPSTER.

❛ The Derby is a national day out for aristocrats and artisans, gypsies and generals, viscounts and villains. ❜

TIM NELIGAN, former Managing Director of Epsom, 1979.

Landmarks and Legends 1942

THE FAVOURITE BIG GAME'S DERBY DEFEAT ROBS KING GEORGE VI OF A CLEAN SWEEP IN THE CLASSICS.

❛ There is something magical about Derby day. It is, and always has been, a day for everyone, and it does not matter what clothes you are dressed in, from morning suits down to singlets and shorts. ❜

Derby-winning trainer PETER WALWYN.

❛ The female contingent on the Derby Day is not the least remarkable part of the London outpouring. Everyone is prepared for 'larks', but the women are even more brilliantly and resolutely prepared than the men; there is no better chance to follow the range of type – not that it is to be called large – of the British female of the lower orders. ❜

HENRY JAMES, 1877.

❛ It [Derby Day] used to be a field day for pickpockets and prostitutes, but now it's simply a good-natured carnival, a shared national experience – and refreshingly classless. Top hats, funfairs and gypsies.

Journalist ANTHONY CLAVANE

Landmarks and Legends 1946

THE DERBY RETURNS TO EPSOM AFTER BEING RUN AT NEWMARKET DURING THE WAR YEARS.

Gazing down [at the first post-war running of the Derby] he saw that the crowd had suddenly parted to let through a long line of disabled men in hospital blue, walking slowly and painfully. The King jerked his hand towards them. 'They have paid the price for us,' he said in his gruff voice. 'Without them there would be no Derby today.

KENNETH ROSE in The Life of King George V.

Absenteeism was passively, if not actively encouraged – if the boss could go to the races, so could the workers. There was always such a mass of humanity at Epsom that the odds against being spotted were astronomical. ❜

GREAT MOMENTS IN RACING.

Landmarks and Legends 1947

THE PHOTO-FINISH CAMERA IS IN OPERATION FOR THE FIRST TIME. 2,000 GUINEAS WINNER TUDOR MINSTREL STARTS AT 4-7, BUT CAN ONLY FINISH FOURTH.

❛ For one mortal hour do we stand on the soaked turf in the pouring rain, with that horrid occasional shiver which always accompanies wet feet, waiting for a start to be effected. Every ten minutes rises a subdued murmur of hope, followed by a growl of disappointment. At last they are really 'off', and for two minutes we forget our misery. But it comes upon us with redoubled force when the race is over, and there is nothing more to look forward to. ❜

CHARLES DICKENS, 1863 – when in torrential rain there were thirty-four false starts before the Derby runners were eventually dispatched.

On the train to Tattenham Corner there was the usual sense of wonder about the willingness of so many people to settle for being somewhere other than Epsom on this afternoon. Glimpses of men hoeing vegetable patches, of women hanging out clothes, or of clerks and executives in dark suits steering briefcases through sweating crowds at East Croydon, evoked a strange presumptuous sympathy.

The physical reality of the Derby is so magical for some of us that we are inclined to feel sorry for anyone who misses out on it. We find it hard to accept that there are millions who are happy to take a less intimate, more ephemeral pleasure from the event, for whom the Derby is a momentary thrill, a fleeting blur of excitement that brightens a working week, a parade watched from office or factory window.

Journalist HUGH MCILVANNEY, 1975.

Landmarks and Legends **1948**

THIRTY-TWO RUNNERS GO TO POST, THE LARGEST DERBY FIELD FOR 86 YEARS.

Derby Day traditionally falls on the first Wednesday in June, when huge crowds always pack the beautiful downs, lining the rails several deep right down to Tattenham Corner. There is a real carnival atmosphere with open-topped buses, fun-fairs, a tented village and plenty of gypsies gazing into their crystal balls. ❞

Author, television broadcaster and seven times champion National Hunt jockey JOHN FRANCOME.

❝ A dull Derbv is looked upon, we believe, as a sort of national calamity. ❞

THE TIMES, 1877.

Landmarks and Legends 1949

THE PHOTO-FINISH IS USED TO DECIDE THE OUTCOME OF THE DERBY FOR THE FIRST TIME. NIMBUS BEATS AMOUR DRAKE AND SWALLOW TAIL BY A HEAD AND THE SAME.

❝ The spectacle, however, is of course an infinitesimally small part of the purpose of Epsom and the interest of the Derby. The finer vibration resides presumably in having money on the affair. ❞

HENRY JAMES, American novelist, about Derby Day 1877.

‘The world and his wife came to Epsom, the gypsies and ‘pearlies’ by ancient custom, the tipsters and the bookmakers for gain, but the majority for a day of fun and bustle and laughter on the Downs, with the occasional glimpse of a famous horse and a famous jockey and a famous racing personage, and at regular times the quick dash of horses’ heads and bright colours as a Derby Day field sweeps by.’

Racing historian BILL CURLING, 1951.

Landmarks and Legends 1951

CHARLIE SPARES, BETTER KNOWN AS A HURDLES JOCKEY, WINS THE DERBY ON HIS FIRST RIDE IN THE RACE ON ARCTIC PRINCE.

‘The whole world was at Epsom yesterday.’

THE TIMES, 1829.

‘The tradition and history behind the Derby, as with the Grand National, are so powerful that I get a cold shiver down my spine every time I go to Epsom, one of the foremost shrines of racing. ❞

Derby-winning trainer PETER WALWYN.

Peter Walwyn

❝ If the weather be fine, there are seldom less than 60,000 assembled here when the Derby Stakes are contested. Of these the vicious and unprincipled form a tolerable proportion . . . ❞

Epsom resident HENRY POWNALL, 1825.

❛ The Derby has its own place in social life for men and women alike. It still remains, however, a race meeting above all things, and not the combination of race and garden party which distinguishes Ascot in particular and Goodwood up to a point. ❜

MRS MASSEY LYON, *Etiquette*, 1927.

'Horses? What Horses?

❛ On Derby Day, a population rolls and surges and scrambles through the place that may be counted in millions. ❜

CHARLES DICKENS, 1851.

Landmarks and Legends 1953

THE CORONATION DERBY. AUREOLE, OWNED BY THE FRESHLY-CROWNED QUEEN, IS SECOND TO PINZA, WHO GIVES THE JUST-KNIGHTED SIR GORDON RICHARDS HIS ONLY DERBY AT HIS TWENTY-EIGHTH ATTEMPT.

‘If the weather be fine, there are seldom less than 60,000 assembled here when the Derby Stakes are contested. Of these the vicious and unprincipled form a tolerable proportion . . .’

Epsom resident HENRY POWNALL, 1825.

Landmarks and Legends 1954

EIGHTEEN-YEAR-OLD LESTER PIGGOTT WINS HIS FIRST DERBY ON 33-1 SHOT NEVER SAY DIE.

‘The air remains thick with gypsy heather on Derby day, as the huge wheel of London's original but now second eye in the funfair near Tattenham Corner dominates the landscape.’

Journalist RICHARD EDMONDSON, 2003.

Landmarks and Legends 1962

SEVEN RUNNERS FALL ON THE DESCENT OF TATTENHAM HILL.

‘On Derby Day London transports itself bodily to Epsom Downs. You scarcely see anything of the rural element at the Derby. The County Families may be there; but they do not affect the airs of provincial supremacy, as they are apt to do at some other race meetings . . .

At Epsom the county element is completely swamped by the town one . . . Belgravia jostles South Lambeth; Capel Court and Pall Mall rub shoulders; a contingent from Bermondsey comes down in the same train with a cohort from Highgate; all ranks and conditions of men and women are jumbled together on the course.’

Journalist GEORGE AUGUSTUS SALA, 1892.

❛ For one reason or another, business or pleasure, a large part of the inhabitants of the civilised world is accustomed to spend some of the leisure hours of the spring picking the Derby winner. It is a blameless pleasure, which has kept more men out of trouble than it has led astray. ❜

GUY GRIFFITH and MICHAEL OAKSHOTT, 1936.

'. . . kept more men out of trouble than it has led astray'

❛ [Derby Day] was extremely low and rowdyish. ❜

HENRY JAMES, 1877.

"Like the Boat Race, Trooping of the Colour and the announcement of another Rolling Stones world tour, Derby Day remains a reassuring ritual for the older generation in a changing world."

TIMEFORM essay, 1998.

Remember Spion Kop? No – the Derby winner, not the campaign!

Landmarks and Legends 1967

FOR THE FIRST TIME THE DERBY IS STARTED BY STARTING STALLS. THE RACE IS WON BY ROYAL PALACE.

❛ Horse-racing and cock-fighting are carried on here to a pitch of absolute madness. There are neither lists nor barriers at these races. The horses run in the midst of the crowd, who leave only a space sufficient for them to pass through, at the same time encouraging them by gestures and loud shouts. ❜

Observations of a French visitor to the Derby in its early years.

❛ Kindly postpone the Derby until 4 p.m. Have missed the train.

Telegram from GRAND DUKE ALEXIS to the Epsom Grandstand Association in 1892. His request was ignored.

❛ The afternoon's entertainment was completed by a traditional four-mile heat race for a £50 purse, and a main of cock-fighting between the birds of 'the Gentlemen of Middlesex and Surrey, and of the Gentlemen of Wiltshire', a contest that doubtless gave as much pleasure as the race itself to Lord Derby (whose devotion to the sport moved him at times to .convert his drawing-room into an impromptu cockpit).

Writer MICHAEL WYNN JONES recalling how the first ever Derby Day was far more than simply seeing which three-year-old could run a mile the fastest.

Landmarks and Legends 1979

THE 200TH RUNNING OF THE DERBY ATTRACTS A CROWD ESTIMATED IN EXCESS OF 500,000.

Back from Epsom yesterday having lost £1,400. Very glad it is all over, and hope to keep clear of it for the future, though as long as I have horses (and there is no getting rid of them) I shall never be able to avoid doing as others do. The example is contagious, and good resolutions are forgotten in some momentary impulse.

Diarist CHARLES GREVILLE, 2 June 1838.

Landmarks and Legends 1983

LESTER PIGGOTT WINS HIS NINTH AND FINAL DERBY ON TEENOSO.

❛ Epsom during the races, and Epsom at any other time, are things as unlike as the Desert of the Saharah and the interior of the Palace of Glass in Hyde Park. ❜

CHARLES DICKENS, 1851.

Landmarks and Legends 1992

THE QUEEN'S STAND IS OPENED ON DERBY DAY BY HER MAJESTY QUEEN ELIZABETH II.

❛ We presently dived into the alleys of the racing ground, and I speedily came to the conclusion that the audience attend principally for the sake of gorging themselves with pigeon pie and lobster salad.

JOHN EVERETT MILLAIS, nineteenth-century artist, on a visit to the Derby in 1853.

Landmarks and Legends 1995

THE DERBY IS SPONSORED BY VODAFONE FOR THE FIRST TIME AND RUN ON A SATURDAY FOR THE FIRST TIME SINCE THE CORONATION DERBY IN 1953. LAMMTARRA WINS IN A RECORD TIME FOR THE RACE OF 2 MINUTES 32.31 SECONDS.

Derby Day is a particularly good day for eels. It is quite early in the eel season and in Victorian times they came up the Thames succulent and delicious, though pollution today means they probably come from Brixham.

LORD LLOYD-WEBBER, 1994.

Landmarks and Legends 1996

ALEX GREAVES BECOMES THE FIRST EVER LADY RIDER IN THE DERBY, FINISHING LAST ON PORTUGUESE LIL.

‘Truth obliges us to state a fact which we trust will never again be our lot, as public journalists, to record, namely that the Queen of England was absolutely in want of a piece of bread. Whether it was that the bracing air of the Downs had sharpened the appetite of her Majesty, or that the caterer for the royal luncheon had been unusuallv stingy in his supply, we cannot take upon ourselves to say.’

BELL'S LIFE commenting on Queen Victoria's unsuccessful and, not surprisingly, only visit to the Derby in 1840.

Landmarks and Legends 2001

GALILEO WINS IN 2 MINUTES 33.27 SECONDS, THE SECOND FASTEST TIME IN THE HISTORY OF THE RACE.

Derby Day was always a bit special. As a child I was fascinated by it – the fun fair, the fortune tellers, the boxing booths, the cockle stalls and the crowds We loved it!

SIR ERNEST HARRISON, who as the former Chairman was the architect of Vodafone's sponsorship of the Derby.

Landmarks and Legends 2002

LEADING STALLION SADLER'S WELLS, HAVING BROKEN HIS DERBY DUCK WITH GALILEO IN 2001 STRIKES AGAIN WITH HIGH CHAPARRAL. BUT TRAGEDY CASTS A CLOUD OVER THE RACE AS COSHOCTON BREAKS A LEG CLOSE HOME AND HAS TO BE DESTROYED.

For once people speak to each other to whom they have never been formally introduced, and positively hob and nob with those palpably inferior to them in station. It is clearly subversive of the proper distinctions which should always in a well-governed society exist between class and class.

A far from politically correct *ILLUSTRATED LONDON NEWS* observing the coming together of the social classes on Derby Day in the late nineteenth century.

Landmarks and Legends 2003

NUMBER OF RUNNERS IN THE DERBY RESTRICTED TO 20 FOR SAFETY REASONS.

‘All persons playing or betting in any booth or public place, at any table or instrument of gaming, or at any game or pretended game of chance, will be taken into custody by the police and may be committed to a House of Correction, and there kept to hard labour for three months.’

Notice, bearing the signature of the Police Superintendent of Scotland Yard, posted at Epsom prior to the running of the 1844 Derby.

‘And so towards Epsom, talking all the way pleasantly. The country very fine, only, the way very dusty. We got to Epsom by eight o'clock to the Well, where much company; and there we alighted and I drank the water; they did not, but did go about and walk a little among the women, but I did drink four pints and had some very good stools by it.’

SAMUEL PEPYS, 14 July 1667, in praise of the efficacy of the Epsom waters, the discovery of which, early in the seventeenth century, led to development of racing there and ultimately the creation of the Derby.

Roll of honour, 1780–2003

	Horse	Trainer	Jockey	SP
1780	Diomed	R. Teasdale	S. Arnull	6-4
(2) Budrow; (3) Spitfire. Owner: Sir C. Bunbury. 9 ran.				
1781	Young Eclipse	——---	C. Hindley	10-1
(2) Crop; (3) Prince Of Orange. Owner: Major D. O'Kelly. 15 ran.				
1782	Assassin	F. Neale	S. Arnull	5-1
(2) Sweet Robin; (3) Fortunio. Owner: Lord Egremont. 13 ran.				
1783	Saltram	F. Neale	C. Hindley	5-2
(2) Dungannon; (3) Parlington. Owner: J. Parker. 6 ran.				
1784	Serjeant	——---	J. Arnull	3-1
(2) Carlo Khan; (3) Dancer. Owner: Colonel D. O'Kelly. 11 ran.				
1785	Aimwell	J. Pratt	C. Hindley	7-1
(2) Grantham; (3) Verjuice. Owner: Lord Clermont. 10 ran.				
1786	Noble	F. Neale	J. White	30-1
(2) Meteor; (3) Clarter. Owner: T. Panton. 15 ran.				

1787 Sir Peter Teazle Saunders S. Arnull 2-1

(2) Gunpowder; (3) Bustler. Owner: Lord Derby. 7 ran.

1788 Sir Thomas F. Neale W. South 5-6

(2) Aurelius; (3) Freenow. Owner: HRH Prince of Wales. 11 ran.

1789 Skyscraper M. Stephenson S. Chifney, sen. 4-7

(2) Sir George: (3) Skylark. Owner: Duke of Bedford. 11 ran.

1790 Rhadamanthus J. Pratt J. Arnull 5-4

(2) Asparagus; (3) Lee Boo. Owner: Lord Grosvenor. 10 ran.

1791 Eager M. Stephenson M. Stephenson 5-2

(2) Vermin; (3) Proteus. Owner: Duke of Bedford. 9 ran.

1792 John Bull J. Pratt F. Buckle 4-6

(2) Speculator; (3) Bustard. Owner: Lord Grosvenor. 7 ran.

1793 Waxy R. Robson W. Clift 12-1

(2) Gohanna; (3) Triptolemus. Owner: Sir F. Poole. 13 ran.

1794 Daedalus J. Pratt F. Buckle 6-1

(2) Ragged Jack; (3) Leon. Owner: Lord Grosvenor. 4 ran.

1795 Spread Eagle R. Prince A. Wheatley 3-1

(2) Caustic; (3) Pelter. Owner: Sir F. Standish. 11 ran.

1796 Didelot | R. Prince | J. Arnull | n/a

(2) Stickler; (3) Leviathan. Owner: Sir F. Standish. 11 ran.

1797 Fidget colt | M. Stephenson | J. Singleton | 10-1

(2) Escalus; (3) Plaistow. Owner: Duke of Bedford. 7 ran.

1798 Sir Harry | F. Neale | S. Arnull | 7-4

(2) Telegraph; (3) Young Spear. Owner: J. Cookson. 10 ran.

1799 Archduke | R. Prince | J. Arnull | 12-1

(2) Gislebert; (3) Eagle. Owner: Sir F. Standish. 11 ran.

1800 Champion | T. Perren | W. Clift | 7-4

(2) Tag; (3) Mystery. Owner C. Wilson. 13 ran.

1801 Eleanor | J. Frost | J. Saunders | 5-4

(2) Colt by Fidget; (3) Remnant. Owner: Sir C. Bunbury. 12 ran.

1802 Tyrant | R.Robson | F. Buckle | 7-1

(2) Young Eclipse; (3) Orlando. Owner: Duke of Grafton. 9 ran.

1803 Ditto | J. Lonsdale | W. Clift | 7-2

(2) Sir Oliver; (3) Brother to Stamford. Owner: Sir H. Williamson. 6 ran.

1804 Hannibal | F. Neale | W. Arnull | 3-1

(2) Pavilion; (3) Hippocampus. Owner: Lord Egremont. 8 ran.

1805	Cardinal Beaufort	R. D. Boyce	D. Fitzpatrick	20-1

(2) Plantagenet; (3) Goth. Owner: Lord Egremont. 15 ran.

1806	Paris	R. Prince	J. Shepherd	5-1

(2) Trafalgar; (3) Hector. Owner: Lord Foley. 12 ran.

1807	Election	R. D. Boyce	J. Arnull	3-1

(2) Giles Scroggins; (2) Coriolanus. Owner: Lord Egremont. 13 ran.

1808	Pan	J. Lonsdale	F. Collinson	25-1

(2) Vandyke; (3) Chester. Owner: Sir H. Williamson. 10 ran.

1809	Pope	R. Robson	T. Goodisson	20-1

(2) Wizard; (3) Salvator. Owner: Duke of Grafton. 10 ran.

1810	Whalebone	R. Robson	W. Clift	2-1

(2) The Dandy; (3) Eccleston. Owner: Duke of Grafton. 11 ran.

1811	Phantom	J. Edwards	F. Buckle	5-1

(2) Magic; (3) Rival. Owner: Sir J. Shelley. 16 ran.

1812	Octavius	R.D. Boyce	W. Arnull	7-1

(2) Sweep; (3) Comus. Owner: R. Ladbroke. 14 ran.

1813	Smolensko	Crouch	T. Goodisson	evens

(2) Caterpillar; (3) Illusion. Owner: Sir C. Bunbury. 12 ran.

1814	Blücher	R.D. Boyce	W. Arnull	5-2

(2) Perchance; (3) Bourbon. Owner: Lord Stawell. 14 ran.

1815	Whisker	R. Robson	T. Goodisson	8-1

(2) Raphael; (3) Busto. Owner: Duke of Grafton. 13 ran.

1816	Prince Leopold	W. Butler	W. Wheatley	20-1

(2) Nectar; (3) Pandour. Owner: H.R.H. Duke of York 11 ran.

1817	Azor	R. Robson	J. Robinson	50-1

(2) Young Wizard; (3) Sylvanus. Owner: J. Payne. 13 ran.

1818	Sam	T. Perren	S. Chifney, jnr.	7-2

(2) Raby; (3) Prince Paul. Owner: T. Thornhill. 16 ran.

1819	Tiresias	R. Prince	W. Clift	5-2

(2) Sultan; (3) Euphrates. Owner: Duke of Portland. 16 ran.

1820	Sailor	W. Chifney	S. Chifney, jnr.	4-1

(2) Abjer; (3) Tiger. Owner: T. Thornhill. 15 ran.

1821	Gustavus	Crouch	S. Day	2-1

(2) Reginald; (3) Sir Huldibrand. Owner: J. Hunter. 13 ran.

1822	Moses	W. Butler	T. Goodisson	6-1

(2) Figaro: (3) Hampden. Owner: Owner: H.R.H. Duke of York. 12 ran.

1823 Emilius R. Robson F. Buckle 11-8

(2) Tancred; (3) Sir Gray. Owner: J.R. Udney. 11 ran.

1824 Cedric J. Edwards J. Robinson 9-2

(2) Osmond; (3) Sir Grey. Owner: Sir J. Shelley. 16 ran

1825 Middleton J. Edwards J. Robinson 7-4

(2) Rufus; (3) Hogarth. Owner: Lord Jersey. 18 ran.

1826 Lap-dog R Stephenson G. Dockeray 50-1

(2) Shakspeare; (3) Dervise. Owner: Lord Egremont. 19 ran.

1827 Mameluke J. Edwards J. Robinson 9-1

(2) Glenartney; (3) Edmund. Owner: Lord Jersey. 23 ran.

1828 Cadland R.D. Boyce J. Robinson 4-1

(2) The Colonel; (3) Ziganee. Owner: Duke of Rutland. 15 ran.
Cadland won the run-off at 5-4 after a dead-heat.

1829 Frederick J. Forth J. Forth 40-1

(2) The Exquisite. (3) Oatlands. Owner: G.W. Gratwicke 17 ran.

1830 Priam W. Chifney S. Day 4-1

(2) Little Red Rover; (3) Mahmoud. Owner: W. Chifney. 22 ran.

1831 Spaniel J. Rogers W. Wheatley 50-1

(2) Riddlesworth; (3) Incubus. Owner: Lord Lowther. 23 ran.

1832	St Giles	J. Webb	W. Scott	3-1

(2) Perion; (3) Trustee. Owner: R. Ridsdale. 22 ran.

1833	Dangerous	I. Sadler	J. Chapple	30-1

(2) Connoisseur; (3) Revenge. Owner: I. Sadler. 25 ran.

1834	Plenipotentiary	G. Payne	P. Conolly	9-4

(2) Shilelagh; (3) Glencoe. Owner: S. Batson. 22 ran.

1835	Mündig	J. Scott	W. Scott	6-1

(2) Ascot. (3) Pelops. Owner: J. Bowes. 14 ran.

1836	Bay Middleton	J. Edwards	J. Robinson	7-4

(2) Gladiator; (3) Venisson. Owner: Lord Jersey. 21 ran.

1837	Phosphorus	J. Doe	G. Edwards	40-1

(2) Caravan; (3) Mahmetan. Owner: Lord Berners. 17 ran.

1838	Amato	R.Sherwood	J. Chapple	30-1

(2) Ion; (3) Grey Momus. Owner: Sir G. Heathcote. 23 ran.

1839	Bloomsbury	W. Ridsdale	S. Templeman	25-1

(2) Deception; (3) Euclid. Owner: W. Ridsdale. 21 ran.

1840	Little Wonder	J. Forth	W. Macdonald	50-1

(2) Launcelot; (3) Discord. Owner: D. Robertson. 17 ran.

1841	Coronation	Painter	P. Conolly	5-2

(2) Van Amburgh; (3) Mustapha Muley. Owner: A.T. Rawlinson. 29 ran.

1842	Attila	J. Scott	W. Scott	5-1

(2) Robert de Gorham; (3) Belcoeur. Owner: Colonel G. Anson. 24 ran.

1843	Cotherstone	J. Scott	W. Scott	13-8

(2) Gorhambury; (3) Sirikol. Owner: J. Bowes 23 ran.

1844	Orlando	W. Cooper	E. Flatman	20-1

(2) Ionian; (3) Bay Momus. Owner: Colonel J. Peel. 29 ran.

1845	The Merry Monarch	J. Forth	F. Bell	----

(2) Annandale; (3) Old England. Owner: G.W. Gratwicke. 31 ran. 15-1 was offered 'Forth's lot'

1846	Pyrrhus the First	J. B. Day	S. Day	8-1

(2) Sir Tatton Sykes; (3) Brocardo. Owner: J. Gully. 27 ran.

1847	Cossack	J. Day Jnr.	S. Templeman	5-1

(2) War Eagle; (3) Van Tromp. Owner: T Pedley. 32 ran.

1848	Surplice	J. Kent Jnr.	S. Templeman	evens

(2) Springy Jack; (3) Shylock. Owner: Lord Clifden. 17 ran.

1849	The Flying Dutchman	J. Fobert	C. Marlow	2-1

(2) Hotspur; (3) Tadmor. Owner: Lord Eglinton. 26 ran.

1850	Voltigeur	R. Hill	J. Marson	16-1

(2) Pitsford; (3) Clincher. Owner: Lord Zetland. 24 ran.

1851	Teddington	A. Taylor Snr.	J. Marson	3-1

(2) Marlborough Buck; (3) Neasham. Owner: Sir J. Hawley. 33 ran.

1852	Daniel O'Rourke	J. Scott	F. Butler	25-1

(2) Barbarian; (3) Chief Baron Nicholson. Owner: J. Bowes. 27 ran.

1853	West Australian	J. Scott	F. Butler	6-4

(2) Sittingbourne; (3) Cineas. Owner: J. Bowes. 28 ran.

1854	Andover	J. Day Jnr.	A. Day	7-2

(2) King Tom; (3) The Hermit. Owner: J. Gully. 27 ran.

1855	Wild Dayrell	J. Rickaby	R. Sherwood	evens

(2) Kingstown; (3) Lord of the Isles. Owner: F. L. Popham. 12 ran.

1856	Ellington	T. Dawson	T. Aldcroft	20-1

(2) Yellow Jack; (3) Cannobie. Owner: Admiral O. Harcourt. 24 ran.

1857	Blink Bonny	W. I'Anson	J. Charlton	20-1

(2) Black Tommy; (3) Adamus. Owner: W. I'Anson. 30 ran.

1858	Beadsman	G. Manning	J. Wells	10-1

(2) Toxophilite; (3) The Hadji. Owner: Sir J. Hawley. 23 ran.

1859 Musjid G. Manning J. Wells 9-4

(2) Marionette; (3) Trumpeter. Sir J. Hawley. 30 ran.

1860 Thormanby M. Dawson H. Custance 4-1

(2) The Wizard; (3) Horror. Owner: J. Merry. 30 ran.

1861 Kettledrum G. Oates R. Bullock 12-1

(2) Dundee; (3) Diophantes. Owner: Colonel C. Towneley. 18 ran.

1862 Caractacus R. Smith J. Parsons 40-1

(2) The Marquis; (3) Buckstone. Owner: C. Snewing. 34 ran.

1863 Macaroni J.K. Godding T. Chaloner 10-1

(2) Lord Clifden; (3) Rapid Rhone. Owner: R.C. Naylor. 31 ran.

1864 Blair Athol W. I'Anson J. Snowden 14-1

(2) General Peel; (3) Scottish Chief. Owner: W.I'Anson. 30 ran.

1865 Gladiateur T. Jennings H. Grimshaw 5-2

(2) Christmas Carol; (3) Eltham. Owner: Count F. de Lagrange. 30 ran.

1866 Lord Lyon J. Dover H. Custance 5-6

(2) Savernake; (3) Rustic. Owner: R Sutton. 26 ran.

1867 Hermit G. Bloss J. Daley 1,000-15

(2) Marksman; (3) Vauban. Owner: H. Chaplin. 30 ran.

1868	Blue Gown	J. Porter	J. Wells	7-2

(2) King Alfred; (3) Speculum. Owner: Sir J. Hawley. 18 ran.

1869	Pretender	T. Dawson	J. Osborne	11-8

(2) Pero Gomez; (3) The Drummer. Owner: J. Johnstone. 22 ran.

1870	Kingcraft	M. Dawson	T. French	20-1

(2) Palmerston; (3) Muster. Owner: Lord Falmouth. 15 ran.

1871	Favonius	J. Hayhoe	M. French	9-1

(2) Albert Victor dead-heated with King of the Forest. Owner: Baron de Rothschild. 17 ran.

1872	Cremorne	W. Gilbert	C. Maidment	3-1

(2) Pell Mell; (3) Queen's Messenger. Owner: H. Savile. 23 ran.

1873	Doncaster	R. Peck	F. Webb	45-1

(2) Gang Forward dead-heated with Kaiser. Owner: J. Merry. 12 ran.

1874	George Frederick	T. Leader	H. Custance	9-1

(2) Couronne de Fer; (3) Atlantic. Owner: W.S. Cartwright. 20 ran.

1875	Galopin	J. Dawson Snr.	J. Morris	2-1

(2) Claremont; (3) Remorse. Owner: Prince Batthyany. 18 ran.

1876	Kisber	J. Hayhoe	C. Maidment	4-1

(2) Forerunner; (3) Julius Caesar. Owner: A. Baltazzi. 15 ran.

1877 Silvio M. Dawson F. Archer 100-9

(2) Glen Arthur; (3) Rob Roy. Owner: Lord Falmouth. 17 ran.

1878 Sefton A. Taylor H. Constable 100-12

(2) Insulaire; (3) Childeric. Owner: W.S. Crawfurd. 22 ran.

1879 Sir Bevys J. Hayhoe G. Fordham 20-1

(2) Palmbearer; (3) Visconti. Owner: Baron L. de Rothschild. 23 ran.

1880 Bend Or R. Peck F. Archer 2-1

(2) Robert the Devil; (3) Mask. Owner: Duke of Westminster. 19 ran.

1881 Iroquois J. Pincus F.Archer 11-2

(2) Peregrine; (3) Town Moor. Owner: P. Lorillard. 15 ran.

1882 Shotover J. Porter T. Cannon 11-2

(2) Quicklime; (3) Sachern. Owner: Duke of Westminster. 14 ran.

1883 St Blaise J. Porter C. Wood 11-2

(2) Highland Chief; (3) Galliard. Owner: Sir F. Johnstone. 12 ran.

1884 St Gatien R. Sherwood C. Wood 100-8

Harvester J. Jewitt S. Loates 100-1

Dead-heat; (3) Queen Adelaide

1885 Melton M. Dawson F. Archer 75-40

(2) Paradox; (3) Royal Hampton. Owner: Lord Hastings. 12 ran.

1886	Ormonde	J. Porter	F. Archer	4-9

(2) The Bard; (3) St Mirin. Owner: Duke of Westminster. 9 ran.

1887	Merry Hampton	M. Gurry	J. Watts	100-9

(2) The Baron; (3) Martley. Owner: G. A. Baird. 11 ran

1888	Ayrshire	G. Dawson	F. Barrett	5-6

(2) Crowberry; (3) Van Dieman's Land. Owner: Duke of Portland. 9 ran.

1889	Donovan	G. Dawson	T. Loates	8-11

(2) Miguel; (3) El Dorado. Owner: Duke of Portland. 13 ran.

1890	Sainfoin	J. Porter	J. Watts	100-15

(2) Le Nord; (3) Orwell. Owner: Sir J. Miller. 8 ran.

1891	Common	J. Porter	G. Barrett	10-11

(2) Gouverneur; (3) Martenhurst. Sir F. Johnstone. 11 ran.

1892	Sir Hugo	T. Wadlow	F. Allsopp	40-1

(2) La Fleche; (3) Bucentaure. Owner: Lord Bradford. 13 ran.

1893	Isinglass	J. Jewitt	T. Loates	4-9

(2) Ravensbury; (3) Raeburn. Owner: H. McCalmont. 11 ran.

1894	Ladas	M. Dawson	J. Watts	2-9

(2) Matchbox; (3) Reminder. Owner: Lord Rosebery. 7 ran.

1895	Sir Visto	M. Dawson	S. Loates	9-1

(2) Curzon; (3) Kirkconnel. Owner: Lord Rosebery. 15 ran.

1896	Persimmon	R. Marsh	J. Watts	5-1

(2) St Frusquin; (3) Earwig. Owner: H.R.H. Prince of Wales 11 ran.

1897	Galtee More	S. Darling	C. Wood	1-4

(2) Velasquez; (3) History. Owner: J Gubbins. 11 ran.

1898	Jeddah	R. Marsh	O. Madden	100-1

(2) Batt; (3) Dunlop. Owner: J.W. Larnach. 18 ran.

1899	Flying Fox	J. Porter	M. Cannon	2-5

(2) Damocles; (3) Innocence. Owner: Duke of Westminster. 12 ran.

1900	Diamond Jubilee	R. Marsh	H. Jones	6-4

(2) Simon Dale; (3) Disguise. Owner: H.R.H. Prince of Wales. 14 ran.

1901	Volodyovski	J. Huggins	L. Reiff	5-2

(2) William the Third; (3) Veronese. Owner: W.C. Whitney. 25 ran.

1902	Ard Patrick	S. Darling	J.H. Martin	100-14

(2) Rising Glass; (3) Friar Tuck. Owner: J. Gubbins. 18 ran.

1903	Rock Sand	G. Blackwell	D. Maher	4-6

(2) Vinicius; (3) Flotsam. Owner: Sir J. Miller. 7 ran.

1904	St Amant	A. Hayhoe	K. Cannon	5-1

(2) John O'Groats; (3) St Denis. Owner: L. de Rothschild. 8 ran.

1905	Cicero	P. Peck	D. Maher	4-11

(2) Jardy; (3) Signorino. Owner: Lord Rosebery. 9 ran.

1906	Spearmint	P. P. Gilpin	D. Maher	6-1

(2) Picton; (3) Troutbeck. Owner: Major E. Loder. 22 ran.

1907	Orby	Colonel F. McCabe (Ireland)	J. Reiff	110-9

(2) Wool Winder; (3) Slieve Gallion. Owner: R. Croker. 9 Ran.

1908	Signorinetta	Chev. E. Ginistrelli	W. Bullock	100-1

(2) Primer; (3) Llangwym. Owner: Chev. E. Ginistrelli. 18 ran.

1909	Minoru	R. Marsh	H. Jones	7-2

(2) Louviers; (3) William the Fourth. Owner: H.M. King Edward VII. 15 ran.

1910	Lemberg	A. Taylor	B. Dillon	7-4

(2) Greenback; (3) Charles O'Malley. Owner: A. W. Cox 15 ran.

1911	Sunstar	C. Morton	G. Stern	13-8

(2) Stedfast; (3) Royal Tender. Owner: J.B. Joel. 26 ran.

1912	Tagalie	D. Waugh	J. Reiff	100-8

(2) Jaeger; (3) Tracery. Owner: W. Raphael. 20 ran.

1913	Aboyeur	T. Lewis	E. Piper	100-1
(2) Louvois; (3) Great Sport. Owner: A.P. Cunliffe. 15 ran.				
1914	Durbar	T. Murphy (France)	M. MacGee	20-1
(2) Hapsburg; (3) Peter the Hermit. Owner: H. Duryea. 30 ran.				
1915*	Pommern	C. Peck	S. Donoghue	11-10
(2) Let Fly; (3) Rossendale. Owner: S.B. Joel. 17 ran.				
1916*	Fifinella	R.C. Dawson	J. Childs	11-2
(2) Kwang-Su; (3) Nassovian. Owner: E. Hulton. 10 ran.				
1917*	Gay Crusader	A. Taylor	S. Donoghue	7-4
(2) Dansellon; (3) Dark Legend. Owner: A. W. Cox. 12 ran.				
1918*	Gainsborough	A. Taylor	J. Childs	8-13
(2) Blink; (3) Treclare. Owner: Lady J. Douglas. 13 ran				
1919	Grand Parade	F. Barling	F. Templeman	33-1
(2) Buchan; (3) Paper Money. Owner: Lord Glanely. 13 ran.				
1920	Spion Kop	P.P. Gilpin	F. O'Neill	100-6
(2) Archaic; (3) Orpheus. Owner: Major G. Loder. 19 ran.				
1921	Humorist	C. Morton	S. Donoghue	6-1
(2) Craig an Eran; (3) Lemonora. Owner: J.B. Joel. 23 ran.				

* Run at Newmarket due to the war

1922	Captain Cuttle	F. Darling	S. Donoghue	10-1

(2) Tamar; (3) Craigangower. Owner: Lord Woolavington. 30 ran.

1923	Papyrus	B. Jarvis	S. Donoghue	100-15

(2) Pharos; (3) Parth. Owner: B. Irish. 19 ran.

1924	Sansovino	Hon. G. Lambton	T. Weston	9-2

(2) St Germans; (3) Hurstwood. Owner: Lord Derby. 27 ran.

1925	Manna	F. Darling	S. Donoghue	9-1

(2) Zionist; (3) The Sirdar. Owner: H.E. Morriss. 27 ran.

1926	Coronach	F. Darling	J Childs	11-2

(2) Lancegaye; (3) Colorado. Owner: Lord Woolavington. 19 ran.

1927	Call Boy	J.E. Watts	E.C. Elliott	4-1

(2) Hot Night; (3) Shian Mor. Owner: F. Curzon. 23 ran.

1928	Felstead	O. Bell	H. Wragg	33-1

(2) Flamingo; (3) Black Watch. Owner: Sir H. Cunliffe-Owen. 19 ran.

1929	Trigo	R. Dawson	J. Marshall	33-1

(2) Walter Gay; (3) Brienz. Owner: W. Barnett. 26 ran.

1930	Blenheim	R. Dawson	H. Wragg	18-1

(2) Iliad; (3) Diolite. Owner: H.H. Aga Khan III. 17 ran.

1931 Cameronian F. Darling F. Fox 7-2

(2) Orpen; (3) Sandwich. Owner: J.A. Dewar. 25 ran.

1932 April The Fifth T. Walls F. Lane 100-6

(2) Dastur; (3) Miracle. Owner: T. Walls. 21 ran.

1933 Hyperion Hon. G. Lambton T. Weston 6-1

(2) King Salmon; (3) Statesman. Owner: Lord Derby. 24 ran.

1934 Windsor Lad M. Marsh C. Smirke 15-2

(2) Easton; (3) Colombo. Owner: H.H. Maharaja of Rajpipla. 19 ran.

1935 Bahram F. Butters F. Fox 5-4

(2) Robin Goodfellow; (3) Field Trial. Owner: H.H. Aga Khan III. 16 ran.

1936 Mahmoud F. Butters C. Smirke 100-8

(2) Taj Akbar; (3) Thankerton. Owner: H.H. Aga Khan III. 22 ran.

1937 Mid-day Sun F.S. Butters M. Beary 100-7

(2) Sandsprite; (3) Le Grand Duc. Owner: Mrs. L. Miller.. 21 ran.

1938 Bois Roussel F. Darling E.C. Elliott 20-1

(2) Scottish Union; (3) Pasch. Owner: P. Beatty. 22 ran.

1939 Blue Peter J. Jarvis E. Smith 7-2

(2) Fox Cub; (3) Heliopolis. Owner: Lord Rosebery. 27 ran.

1940* Pont l'Eveque F. Darling S. Wragg 10-1

(2) Turkhan; (3) Lighthouse. Owner: F. Darling. 16 ran.

1941* Owen Tudor F. Darling W. Nevett 25-1

(2) Morogoro; (3) Firoze Din. Owner: Mrs C. Macdonald-Buchanan. 20 ran.

1942* Watling Street W. Earl H. Wragg 6-1

(2) Hyperides; (3) Ujiji. Owner: Lord Derby. 13 ran.

1943* Straight Deal W. Nightingall T.H. Carey 100-6

(2) Umiddad; (3) Nasrullah. Owner: Miss D. Paget. 23 ran.

1944* Ocean Swell Sir J. Jarvis W. Nevett 28-1

(2) Tehran; (3) Happy Landing. Owner: Lord Rosebery. 20 ran.

1945* Dante M. Peacock W. Nevett 100-30

(2) Midas; (3) Court Martial. Owner: E. Ohlson. 27 ran.

1946 Airborne R. Perryman T. Lowrey 50-1

(2) Gulf Stream; (3) Radiotherapy. 1 length, 2 lengths. Owner: J.E. Ferguson. 17 ran.

1947 Pearl Diver P. Carter (France) G. Bridgland 40-1

(2) Migoli; (3) Sayajirao. 4 lengths, threequarters of a length. Owner: Baron G. de Waldner 15 ran.

1948 My Love R. Carver (France) W. Johnstone 100-9

(2) Royal Drake; (3) Noor. One and a half lengths, 4 lengths. Owner: H.H. Aga Khan III. 32 ran.

* Run at Newmarket due to the war

1949 Nimbus G.S. Colling E.C. Elliott 7-1

(2) Amour Drake; (3) Swallow Tail. Head, same. Owner: Mrs M. Glenister. 32 ran.

1950 Galcador C.H. Semblat (France) W. Johnstone 100-9

(2) Prince Simon; (3) Double Eclipse. Head, 4 lengths. Owner: M. Boussac. 25 ran.

1951 Arctic Prince W. Stephenson C. Spares 28-1

(2) Sybil's Nephew; (3) Signal Box. 6 lengths, head. Owner: J. McGrath. 33 ran.

1952 Tulyar M. Marsh C. Smirke 11-2

(2) Gay Time; (3) Faubourg. Threequarters of a length, 1 length. Owner: H.H. Aga Khan III. 33 ran.

1953 Pinza N. Bertie Sir G. Richards 5-1

(2) Aureole; (3) Pink Horse. 4 lengths, one and a half lengths. Owner: Sir V. Sassoon. 27 ran.

1954 Never Say Die J. Lawson L. Piggott 33-1

(2) Arabian Night; (3) Darius. 2 lengths, neck. Owner: R.S. Clark. 22 ran.

1955 Phil Drake F. Mathet (France) F. Palmer 100-8

(2) Panaslipper; (3) Acropolis. One and a half lengths, 3 lengths. Owner: Mme S. Volterra. 23 ran.

1956 Lavandin A. Head (France) W. Johnstone 7-1

(2) Montaval; (3) Roistar. Neck, 2 lengths. Owner: P. Wertheimer. 27 ran.

1957 Crepello N. Murless L. Piggott 6-4

(2) Ballymoss; (3) Pipe Of Peace. One and a half lengths, 1 length. Owner: Sir V. Sassoon. 22 ran.

1958 Hard Ridden J. Rogers (Ireland) C. Smirke 18-1

(2) Paddy's Point; (3) Nagami. 5 lengths, one and a half lengths. Sir V. Sassoon. 20 ran.

1959 Parthia C. Boyd-Rochfort W.H. Carr 10-1

(2) Fidalgo; (3) Shantung. One and a half lengths, same. Owner: Sir H. de Trafford. 20 ran.

1960 St Paddy N. Murless L. Piggott 7-1

(2) Alcaeus; (3) Kythnos. 3 lengths, half a length. Owner: Sir V. Sassoon. 17 ran.

1961 Psidium H. Wragg R. Poincelet 66-1

(2) Dicta Drake; (3) Pardao. 2 lengths, neck. Owner: Mrs E. Plesch. 28 ran.

1962 Larkspur M.V. O'Brien (Ireland) N. Sellwood 22-1

(2) Arcor; (3) Le Cantilien. 2 lengths, half a length. Owner: R.R. Guest. 26 ran.

1963 Relko F. Mathet (France) Y. Saint-Martin 5-1

(2) Merchant Venturer; (3) Ragusa. 6 lengths, 3 lengths. Owner: F. Dupré. 26 ran.

1964 Santa Claus J. Rogers (Ireland) A. Breasley 15-8

(2) Indiana; (3) Dilettante. 1 length, 2 lengths. Owner: J. Ismay. 17 ran.

1965 Sea-Bird E. Pollet (France) T.P. Glennon 7-4

(2) Meadow Court; (3) I Say. 2 lengths, one and a half lengths. Owner: J. Ternynck. 22 ran.

1966 Charlottown G. Smyth A. Breasley 5-1

(2) Pretendre; (3) Black Prince. Neck, 5 lengths. Owner: Lady Z. Wernher. 25 ran.

1967	Royal Palace	N. Murless	G.Moore	7-4

(2) Ribocco; (3) Dart Board. Two and a half lengths, 2 lengths. Owner: H. J. Joel. 22 ran.

1968	Sir Ivor	M.V. O'Brien (Ireland)	L. Piggott	4-5

(2) Connaught; (3) Mount Athos. One and a half lengths, two and a half lengtts. Owner: R.R. Guest. 13 ran.

1969	Blakeney	A.M. Budgett	E. Johnson	15-2

(2) Shoemaker; (3) Prince Regent. One length, same. Owner: A.M. Budgett. 26 ran.

1970	Nijinsky	M.V. O'Brien (Ireland)	L. Piggott	11-8

(2) Gyr; (3) Stintino. Two and a half lengths, 3 lengths. Owner: C.W. Engelhard. 11 ran.

1971	Mill Reef	I. Balding	G. Lewis	100-30

(2) Linden Tree; (3) Irish Ball. 2 Lengths, two and a half. Owner: P. Mellon. 21 ran.

1972	Roberto	M.V. O'Brien (Ireland)	L. Piggott	3-1

(2) Rheingold; (3) Pentland Firth. Short head, 3 lengths. Owner: J.W. Galbreath. 22 ran.

1973	Morston	A.M. Budgett	E. Hide	25-1

(2) Cavo Doro; (3) Freefoot. Half a length, two and a half lengths. Owner: A.M. Budgett. 25 ran.

1974	Snow Knight	P. Nelson	B. Taylor	50-1

(2) Imperial Prince; (3) Giacometti. 2 lengths, 1 length. Owner: Mrs S. Phillips. 18 ran.

1975	Grundy	P. Walwyn	Pat Eddery	5-1

(2) Nobiliary; (3) Hunza Dancer. 3 lengths, four lengths. Owner: Dr. C. Vittadini. 18 ran.

1976 Empery M. Zilber (France) L. Piggott 10-1

(2) Relkino; (3) Oats. 3 lengths, head. Owner: N.B. Hunt. 23 ran.

1977 The Minstrel M.V. O'Brien (Ireland) L. Piggott 5-1

(2) Hot Grove: (3) Blushing Groom. Neck, 5 lengths. Owner: R. Sangster. 22 ran.

1978 Shirley Heights J. Dunlop G. Starkey 8-1

(2) Hawaiian Sound; (3) Remainder Man. Head, one and a half lengths. Owner: Lord Halifax. 25 ran.

1979 Troy W.R. Hern W. Carson 6-1

(2) Dickens Hill; (3) Northern Baby. 7 lengths, 3 lengths. Owner: Sir M. Sobell. 23 ran.

1980 Henbit W.R. Hern W. Carson 7-1

(2) Master Willie; (3) Rankin. Half a length, one and a half lengths. Owner: Mrs E. Plesch. 24 ran.

1981 Shergar M. Stoute W.R. Swinburn 10-11

(2) Glint Of Gold; (3) Scintillating Air. 10 lengths, 2 lengths. Owner: H.H. Aga Khan IV. 18 ran.

1982 Golden Fleece M.V. O'Brien (Ireland) Pat Eddery 3-1

(2) Touching Wood; (3) Silver Hawk. 3 lengths, 1 length. Owner: R. Sangster. 18 ran.

1983 Teenoso G. Wragg L.Piggott 9-2

(2) Carlingford Castle; (3) Shearwalk. 3 lengths, same. Owner: E.B. Moller. 21 ran.

1984 Secreto D.V. O'Brien (Ireland) C. Roche 14-1

(2) El Gran Senor; (3) Mighty Flutter. Short head, 3 lengths. Owner: L. Miglietti. 17 ran.

1985	Slip Anchor	H. Cecil	S. Cauthen	9-4

(2) Law Society; (3) Damister. 7 lengths, 6 lengths. Owner: Lord Howard de Walden. 14 ran.

1986	Shahrastani	M. Stoute	W.R. Swinburn	11-2

(2) Dancing Brave; (3) Mashkour. Half a length, two and a half lengths. Owner: H.H. Aga Khan IV. 17 ran.

1987	Reference Point	H. Cecil	S. Cauthen	6-4

(2) Most Welcome; (3) Bellotto. One and a half lengths, short head. Owner: L. Freedman. 19 ran.

1988	Kahyasi	L. Cumani	R. Cochrane	11-1

(2) Glacial Storm; (3) Doyoun. One and a half lengths, same. Owner: H.H. Aga Khan IV. 14 ran.

1989	Nashwan	W.R. Hern	W. Carson	5-4

(2) Terimon; (3) Cacoethes. 5 lengths, 2 lengths. Owner: Sheikh H. Al-Maktoum. 12 ran.

1990	Quest For Fame	R. Charlton	Pat Eddery	7-1

(2) Blue Stag; (3) Elmaamul. 3 lengths, one and a half lengths. Owner: K. Abdullah. 18 ran.

1991	Generous	P. Cole	A. Munro	9-1

(2) Marju; (3) Star Of Gdansk. 5 lengths, 7 lengths. Owner: F. Salman. 13 ran.

1992	Dr Devious	P. Chapple-Hyam	J. Reid	8-1

(2) St Jovite; (3) Silver Wisp. 2 lengths, short head. Owner: S.H. Craig. 18 ran.

1993	Commander In Chief	H. Cecil	M. Kinane	15-2

(2) Blue Judge; (3) Blues Traveller. Three and a half lengths, two and a half lengths. Owner: K. Abdullah. 16 ran.

1994	Erhaab	J. Dunlop	W. Carson	7-2

(2) King's Theatre; (3) Colonel Collins. One and a quarter lengths, one and a half lengths. owner: Sheikh H. Al-Maktoum. 25 ran.

1995	Lammtarra	Saeed Bin Suroor	W.R. Swinburn	14-1

(2) Tamure; (3) Presenting. 1 length, threequarters of a length. Owner: Saeed bin Maktoum Al Maktoum. 15 ran.

1996	Shaamit	W. Haggas	M. Hills	12-1

(2) Dushyantor; (3) Santou. One and a quarter lengths, same. Owner: K. Dasmal. 20 ran.

1997	Benny The Dip	J. Gosden	W. Ryan	11-1

(2) Silver Patriarch; (3) Romanov. Short head, 5 lengths. Owner: L. Knight. 13 ran.

1998	High-Rise	L. Cumani	O. Peslier	20-1

(2) City Honours; (3) Border Arrow. Head, two and a half lengths. Owner: Sheikh Mohammed Obain 15 ran.

1999	Oath	H. Cecil	K. Fallon	13-2

(2) Daliapour; (3) Beat All. One and threequarter lengths, one and a half lengths. Owner: The Thoroughbred Corporation. 16 ran.

2000	Sinndar	J. Oxx (Ireland)	J. Murtagh	7-1

(2) Sakhee; (3) Beat Hollow. 1 length, 5 lengths. Owner: H.H. Aga Khan IV. 15 ran.

2001	Galileo	A. O'Brien (Ireland)	M. Kinane	11-4

(2) Golan; (3) Tobougg. Three and a half lengths, neck. Owner: Mrs S. Magnier & M. Tabor. 15 ran.

2002	High Chaparral	A. O'Brien (Ireland)	J. Murtagh	7-2

(2) Hawk Wing; (3) Moon Ballad. 2 lengths, 12 lengths. Owner: M. Tabor & Mrs S. Magnier. 12 ran.

2003	Kris Kin	Sir Michael Stoute	K. Fallon	6-1

(2) The Great Gatsby; (3) Alamshar. 1 length, short head. Owner: Saeed Suhail. 20 ran.

Select Bibliography

The Derby, Alastair Burnet with Tim Neligan (Michael O'Mara Books – 1993)

The Derby, Michael Wynn Jones (Croom Helm – 1979)

Derby 200, Michael Seth-Smith and Roger Mortimer (Guinness Superlatives – 1979)

Derby Day 200, Patricia Connor and Lionel Lambourne (1979)

The Book of Racing Quotations, Nick Robinson and Sir David Llewellyn (Stanley Paul – 1988)

The Derby 1919 –1947, George Melton (Knapp, Drewett & Sons – 1947)

The Epsom Derby, Roger Mortimer with Tim Neligan (Michael Joseph – 1984)

Epsom Racecourse – Its Story and its People, David Hunn (Davis-Poynter – 1973)

The Faber Book of The Turf, John Hislop and David Swannell (Faber and Faber – 1990)

The History of the Derby Stakes, Roger Mortimer (Cassell – 1961)

British Racecourses, B.W.R. Curling (H.F. & G. Witherby Ltd. – 1951)

The Romance of the Derby Stakes, Alan Macey (Hutchinson & Co. (Publishers) Ltd. – 1930)

Runners and Riders – An Anthology of Writing on Racing, Edited by Sean Magee (Methuen – 1993)

Index